VEGE

COOKBOOK FOR

BEGINNERS 2024

A Step-by-Step Guide to Delicious Plant-Powered Cooking – more than 70 Easy Recipes for a Tasty Transition.

LUCAS VERDURA

Copyright Lucas Verdura © 2023,

All Rights Reserved.

TABLE OF CONTENTS

Introduction 4

Chapter 1: Introduction to Vegetarianism 9

Chapter 2: Essential Cooking Techniques ... 73

Chapter 3: Building Blocks of Flavor 85

Chapter 4: Breakfast and Brunch Delights ... 91

Chapter 5: Wholesome Lunches 160

Chapter 6: Nourishing Dinners 234

Chapter 7: Snacks and Appetizers 315

Conclusion 347

Introduction

I am excited to introduce you to the exciting world of vegetarian cooking! This cookbook is your necessary guide to embracing a delicious, nutritious, and fulfilling vegetarian lifestyle. Whether you're making the transition to meatless meals for health, ethical, or environmental reasons, this cookbook is your essential guide to making the transition.

A turning point, or a purposeful choice to explore a world of various flavors, plant-based nourishment, and creative cooking, is marked by the decision to embrace a vegetarian diet for many people. This book acts as your compass, guiding you through this process with a wealth of recipes, pointers, and fundamental insights into the art of vegetarian cooking.

The reasons people decide to adopt a vegetarian diet and way of life are as varied as the dishes contained in these pages. Some people are interested in plant-based diets since they have discovered that following such a diet can lower their chance of developing chronic diseases while still providing them with an adequate amount of nutrients and vitality. Others are moved by the ethical and environmental ramifications, knowing the impact that dietary choices have on both the well-being of animals and the continued viability of our planet.

This culinary landscape may initially appear to be intimidating, but there is no need to be afraid because this book has been written specifically for people who are just starting. It is your starting point, packed with core knowledge, vital skills, and a multitude of tasty dishes meant to make your transition to vegetarianism a seamless and pleasurable experience. It is your starting point.

In the next chapters, you will learn how to properly prepare vegetables, how to master the art of blending herbs and spices to enhance flavors, and how to become an expert at preparing meals that are not only nutritionally sound but also delicious to the senses.

Prepare yourself for this voyage by keeping an open mind and an inquisitive palette. There is a recipe suitable for every event and every level of competence, whether you are looking for ideas for hefty dinners, delectable sweets, savory snacks, or breakfast dishes to inspire you in the morning.

Remember, as you embark on this journey through the world of cuisine, that cooking is more than just a set of skills; it is also an act of nurturing and sharing. Experiment, take pleasure in, and celebrate the pleasures of wholesome eating with the people you care about most by eating these meals together.

Are you prepared to plunge into the intricate web of flavors that is vegetarian cuisine? Put on your apron and get your knives in tip-top shape, because we're about to embark on a culinary journey that will not only result in the creation of mouthwatering dishes but also the development of a deeper appreciation for the diverse and abundant world of plant-based cuisine.

We are excited to have you join us on this first tasty step of your journey into the world of vegetarian cooking. Let's make some wonderful dinners out of some fresh, vivid produce that will not only satisfy the senses but also replenish the soul.

Chapter 1

Introduction to Vegetarianism

Why Choose Vegetarianism?

There are numerous reasons why people choose vegetarianism, extending from personal health to ethical, environmental, and even spiritual considerations. Let's delve into these aspects in detail:

Health Benefits

- Reduced Risk of Chronic Diseases: Studies suggest that a well-planned vegetarian diet can lower the risk of heart disease, hypertension, type 2 diabetes, and certain cancers.

- Weight Management: Vegetarian diets, when balanced and properly planned, can aid in weight loss and weight management due to the emphasis on whole foods, fruits, vegetables, and fiber-rich foods.

- Nutrient-Rich Diet: A vegetarian diet can be rich in essential nutrients like fiber, antioxidants, vitamins C and E, magnesium, and potassium.

Ethical Considerations

- Animal Welfare: Many individuals choose vegetarianism due to concerns about animal welfare and the treatment of animals in the food industry.

- Reduction of Animal Suffering: Avoiding meat consumption reduces demand, potentially leading to fewer animals raised in factory farming conditions, which are often associated with cramped spaces and harsh treatment.

Environmental Impact

- Reduced Carbon Footprint: Livestock farming contributes significantly to greenhouse gas emissions. By choosing a vegetarian diet, individuals can reduce their carbon footprint.
- Conservation of Resources: Producing plant-based foods generally requires fewer resources

like water and land compared to raising animals for meat.

Spiritual and Cultural Reasons

- Religious Beliefs: In some religions, such as Hinduism and Jainism, vegetarianism is advocated as a way of life.
- Cultural Traditions: Many cultures have vegetarian dishes as a staple part of their cuisine, which influences dietary choices.

Global Food Security

- Efficient Use of Resources: Vegetarian diets require fewer resources, making it a potentially more sustainable way to feed a growing global population.

- Accessible and Affordable: In certain regions, plant-based foods are more accessible and affordable than meat, making vegetarianism a practical choice for many.

Personal Choice and Taste Preferences

- Preference for Plant-Based Foods: Some individuals simply prefer the taste and variety of plant-based foods over meat.
- Health Consciousness: Personal health concerns or dietary restrictions might lead individuals to choose a vegetarian diet for improved well-being.

Challenges and Considerations

- Nutritional Balance: While vegetarian diets can be nutritious, ensuring a well-balanced intake of nutrients like protein, iron, zinc, calcium, and vitamin B12 is crucial.

- Social and Cultural Challenges: Depending on the cultural and social environment, being vegetarian may present challenges in finding suitable food options or social acceptance.

Ultimately, choosing vegetarianism is a deeply personal decision influenced by a combination of health, ethical, environmental, and cultural factors. The reasons can vary widely from person to person, and some might choose a semi-vegetarian or flexitarian approach, incorporating occasional meat consumption while predominantly following a plant-based diet.

Health benefits

Because of the many positive effects it has on one's health, the vegetarian diet, which abstains from eating meat, poultry, and even fish in some cases, has garnered a lot of attention in recent years. It comprises a variety of subcategories, such as lacto-vegetarian, which consumes dairy products, ovo-vegetarian, which consumes eggs, lacto-ovo-vegetarian, which consumes both dairy and eggs, and vegan, which does not consume any items derived from animals. This decision in food is connected to a variety of benefits that span the well-being of the body, the mind, and the environment.

To begin, switching to a vegetarian diet has been shown to improve one's general health by lowering one's probability of developing chronic diseases. Studies have indicated that vegetarians have a lower risk of developing obesity, hypertension, type 2 diabetes, and cardiovascular diseases than people who don't follow a vegetarian diet. In a vegetarian diet, the consumption of whole plant-based foods, such as fruits, vegetables, legumes, nuts, and whole grains, is prioritized. These foods are excellent sources of fiber, important nutrients, and antioxidants. These factors help to promote heart health by lowering cholesterol levels, regulating blood pressure more effectively, and overall contributing to a lower chance of developing cardiovascular disease.

In addition, the high fiber content of plant-based diets makes digestion easier and improves the health of the digestive tract. It promotes regular bowel movements, helps prevent constipation, and supports a diverse and flourishing gut flora, all of which are important for the regulation of general immunity and inflammation. In addition, there is some speculation that substituting plant proteins for animal proteins in one's diet may be associated with a reduced risk of developing some malignancies, such as colorectal cancer.

A well-known benefit of the vegetarian diet is its potential to aid in both the management and reduction of excess body fat. Plant-based diets often have fewer calories and less saturated fat, but they are also higher in fiber and complex carbohydrates. This combination may assist individuals in experiencing feelings of fullness and satisfaction despite consuming a lower total amount of calories, which may in turn promote both weight loss and the maintenance of a healthy weight.

There is a correlation between eating a plant-based diet and enhanced mental well-being. Some studies have found that plant-based diets may lower the risk of mental health issues like depression and anxiety. However, more study needs to be done in this area. It is possible that the consumption of specific nutrients, such as folate, which is plentiful in leafy greens, and antioxidants, which are found in fruits and vegetables, contributes to the maintenance of good mental health by regulating neurotransmitters and lowering the levels of oxidative stress.

Vegetarianism is also related to positive effects on the surrounding natural environment. The raising of livestock is a major contributor to the generation of greenhouse gases, the destruction of forests, and the consumption of water. If an individual switches to a vegetarian diet, there will be less of a desire for meat, which will result in a smaller amount of carbon dioxide produced by that individual. It does this by conserving resources and avoiding environmental deterioration, both of which are linked to intensive animal agriculture. This helps foster sustainability.

On the other hand, it is crucial to keep in mind that following a well-planned vegetarian diet is necessary to guarantee an adequate consumption of critical elements, some of which may be more easily accessible in animal products. Vitamin B12, iron, calcium, omega-3 fatty acids, and zinc are examples of nutrients that could be lacking in the diet of a vegetarian who does not carefully plan their meals. However, these deficits can be controlled by the use of foods that have been fortified, supplements, and a wide variety of plant-based sources that are abundant in these nutrients.

For example, even though it is most commonly found in animal products, vitamin B12 can also be received in the form of supplements and fortified meals such as cereals and plant-based milk. Iron, which is essential for the circulation of oxygen throughout the body, can be obtained from foods such as beans, tofu, spinach, and grains that have been fortified. Calcium, which is essential for maintaining healthy bones, can be gained by consuming plant-based milk that has been fortified with calcium, tofu, almonds, and leafy green vegetables like kale and collard greens. Flaxseeds, chia seeds, walnuts, and algae-based supplements are all good sources of omega-3 fatty acids, which are critical for maintaining healthy brain function. Whole grains, legumes, nuts, and seeds are all good sources of the mineral zinc, which is essential for immune system function and the healing of wounds.

A well-planned vegetarian diet can offer a range of health benefits, ranging from a decreased chance of developing chronic diseases to an increased likelihood of preserving the health of the environment. However, it is essential to pay close attention to satisfying nutritional needs to guarantee that those who consume a vegetarian diet get all of the necessary elements for achieving their best possible state of health. It is possible to have a nourishing life as a vegetarian, which is beneficial to both one's well-being and the preservation of the natural world, provided one takes the time to arrange their diet carefully.

Environmental impact

The decision to follow a vegetarian diet has repercussions that are far-reaching for the environment, touching on a variety of issues relating to sustainability, resource conservation, and the overall ecological balance of the planet. When assessing the impact that vegetarianism has on the environment, it is necessary to investigate how it influences land use, water conservation, emissions of greenhouse gases, biodiversity, and overall ecological sustainability.

A vegetarian diet has some positive effects on the environment, one of the most significant of which is a decreased need for land resources. The cultivation of livestock, in particular beef cattle, necessitates the use of enormous tracts of land for grazing and the cultivation of feed crops. The conversion of natural habitats and forests into croplands or pastures to provide animal feed is a substantial contributor to the destruction of natural habitats and forests. Individuals can lessen the impact they have on the environment by providing indirect support for deforestation and can contribute to the preservation of important ecosystems and biodiversity by switching to a vegetarian diet.

In addition, when products based on plants are contrasted with those based on animals, the question of which uses the land more efficiently emerges. When compared to the same quantity of protein that can be obtained from plants, the production of one pound of meat requires a much greater amount of space, water, and other resources. When compared to the quantity of land, water, and feed crops required to produce a similar amount of plant-based protein sources like legumes or grains, the amount of land, water, and crops needed to produce one pound of beef demands several times the amount. Because plant-based agriculture has a much greater rate of resource utilization efficiency than animal-based agriculture, vegetarianism is a more environmentally friendly lifestyle choice in terms of land consumption.

Another vitally important factor that can be affected by food decisions is water conservation. The process of raising livestock requires a significant amount of water since animals need large amounts of it to drink, crops need it to be irrigated, and feed needs to be produced. Individuals make an indirect contribution to the movement to conserve water when they cut back on their consumption of products derived from animals. Plant-based diets often have a smaller impact on the environment's water supply since the cultivation of crops for direct human use requires less water than the cultivation of crops to feed animals.

The production of food has a wide-ranging impact on the environment, including emissions of greenhouse gases. The raising of livestock, and cattle farming in particular, is a significant contributor to emissions of greenhouse gases, most notably methane and nitrous oxide. Methane is a potent greenhouse gas that is created during the digestive processes of ruminant animals. In terms of its potential to contribute to global warming, methane is substantially more powerful than carbon dioxide over a shorter period. Individuals can minimize their carbon footprint and mitigate the impact of greenhouse gas emissions linked with animal agriculture by limiting the amount of meat they consume.

In addition to this, the question of how efficiently energy is used comes into play. When compared to the production of plant-based foods, the production of foods derived from animals involves a greater amount of energy inputs, including the use of fossil fuels for the production of feed, transportation, and processing. Individuals can also contribute to overall energy conservation and reduce their dependency on fossil fuels by adopting a vegetarian diet, which in turn lowers the demand for energy-intensive agricultural activities.

The agricultural methods that are involved with the production of meat are a major factor in the loss of biodiversity, which is a major problem. Intensive livestock farming can frequently result in the destruction of habitats and the loss of biodiversity as a consequence of deforestation, soil degradation, and pollution caused by concentrated animal feeding operations (CAFOs). Individuals can assist in lessening the pressure that is being placed on natural ecosystems and contribute to the preservation of biodiversity by adopting a vegetarian diet. This will reduce the need for land conversion and will minimize the environmental problems that are connected with industrial animal agriculture.

In addition, the positive effects of vegetarianism on the environment go beyond the direct effects it has on the land, water, and air. In addition to that, they incorporate the protection of marine resources. The overexploitation of fish resources and the use of fishing methods that are not compatible with sustainable fishing have contributed to the depletion of fish populations and the disruption of marine ecosystems. A reduction in the demand for seafood products can help ease the pressure that is being placed on oceanic ecosystems and supports sustainable fisheries management methods. This is especially true for individuals who choose to abstain from seafood when following a vegetarian diet.

Even though it's common knowledge that vegetarianism is better for the environment, there's still a critical need to recognize the complexities of our food systems and the importance of developing holistic solutions to the problems of environmental sustainability. The adoption of regenerative agricultural practices, the reduction of food waste, and the promotion of sustainable agriculture are all essential aspects of an all-encompassing strategy for the protection of the natural environment.

Additionally, the concept of a "flexitarian diet," which emphasizes the occasional or modest intake of animal products coupled with a diet that is largely plant-based, can also contribute favorably to both an individual's health and the environmental sustainability of the planet. By taking this strategy, individuals can lessen the influence they have on the environment while retaining some leeway in the nutritional decisions they make.

The impact of a vegetarian diet on the environment is multi-faceted and spans across a variety of different aspects of sustainable living. Individuals can greatly lessen their ecological footprint, help preserve natural resources, minimize their contribution to the production of greenhouse gases, and add to the protection of biodiversity if they opt for plant-based diets rather than items derived from animals. However, to achieve total environmental sustainability, collective efforts must be made that involve changes in legislation, technology improvements, and human dietary choices. These changes are intended to foster a food system that is more sustainable and robust for future generations.

Ethical considerations

The adoption of a vegetarian diet is frequently accompanied by ethical issues that extend beyond concerns regarding one's health and the surrounding environment. The care of animals, moral standards, and the treatment of animals used in food production are frequently at the center of discussions among individuals who choose a vegetarian lifestyle out of ethical concerns. This choice in diet originates from a desire to lessen or do away with the exploitation, suffering, and killing of animals for the sake of satisfying one's appetite for food.

The idea of being kind and compassionate to all living things, including animals, lies at the core of vegetarianism's moral justification. Many people who choose to follow a vegetarian diet do so because they are compassionate and because they believe it is morally important to avoid causing any kind of pain or suffering to sentient beings. They disagree with the concept of exploiting animals as commodities or resources for the benefit of humans since they acknowledge that animals are capable of feeling pain and emotions and have a strong desire to survive.

The industrialization of the production of meals derived from animals frequently involves ethically questionable actions. A fundamental moral problem that exists within the food industry is factory farming, which includes practices such as intensive confinement, overcrowding, and the brutal treatment of animals. Animals that are grown for their meat are frequently subjected to stressful and unpleasant living conditions. They are also frequently prevented from engaging in their normal behaviors and given antibiotics and hormones to speed up their growth. These behaviors are regarded as immoral by a significant number of vegetarians, which is what drives them to forgo the use of any items derived from animals.

In addition, the procedure of slaughtering animals for their meat being consumed by humans creates moral and ethical concerns regarding how animals are treated and the repercussions of taking their lives for human consumption. People who advocate for the rights of animals and their freedom from exploitation may hold the position that it is unethical to slaughter animals for food, even if they are kept in humane conditions. This is true even if the animals are killed for their meat.

Some different approaches to morality, like as utilitarianism, deontology, and the notion of animal rights, are compatible with vegetarianism. Because it lessens the amount of anguish that is caused to animals during the production of food, vegetarianism is supported by the utilitarian philosophy of utilitarianism, which seeks to maximize total happiness while minimizing suffering. Individuals may have a moral obligation to refrain from inflicting needless harm to animals; hence, deontological ethics, which emphasizes moral responsibilities and principles, may support a vegetarian way of life as a result of this argument. Animal rights theory, which holds that animals possess inherent rights and ought to be treated with respect and regard, is a staunch advocate for the ethical treatment of animals and frequently correlates with the ideas of vegetarianism. Animal rights theory postulates that animals possess inherent rights and ought to be treated with respect and concern.

In addition, the ethical considerations involved with vegetarianism go beyond the treatment of animals and embrace the broader societal ramifications of the lifestyle. The moral decision to abstain from the consumption of animal products can be interpreted as a stand against the commercialization of living beings, which contributes to the development of a society that is more compassionate and empathic. It advocates a movement away from food systems that are less ethical and sustainable and toward ones that are more ethical and sustainable, and it opposes the prevalent norms and behaviors that consider animals primarily as resources for human consumption.

Ethical issues of vegetarianism, on the other hand, require taking into account not just cultural but also social and economic factors. Traditions and practices within a culture have a significant impact on an individual's food preferences since these traditions and practices are firmly rooted in the individual's diet. Even while navigating one's ethical issues, an individual must demonstrate sensitivity and empathy toward other cultural viewpoints on food and dietary choices. This is necessary to respect the diversity of cultures.

In addition, the availability and cost of foods derived from plants might be ethical concerns for certain people. It may be difficult to get your hands on a wide variety of reasonably priced plant-based foods in some parts of the world or under particular socioeconomic conditions. To address these inequalities, it is necessary to make efforts to promote food equity, enhance accessibility to nutrient-dense plant-based options, and support sustainable food production systems that place a priority on the cost and availability of vegetarian alternatives.

The idea of food sovereignty, as well as the right of individuals and communities to determine their food systems, is yet another factor to take into consideration when it comes to ethics. When promoting vegetarianism, it is imperative to show respect for the liberty that individuals have in determining their dietary choices and to ensure that ethical advocacy does not impose beliefs or interfere with the autonomy of cultural practices.

Concerns for animal welfare, moral standards, societal values, and cultural viewpoints are just a few of the areas that are encompassed by the myriad of ethical factors to be considered before deciding to adopt a vegetarian diet. A desire to live following one's moral principles is reflected in the practice of vegetarianism, which is driven by a dedication to non-violence towards animals and ethical treatment in the production of food. It is crucial to consider cultural variety, accessibility, and respect for individual autonomy while working toward the development of a more ethical and sustainable food system. This is especially true when advocating for ethical dietary choices. The moral perspective that underpins vegetarianism serves as a jumping-off point for conversations about compassion, conscious consumption, and the interdependence of individual decisions with greater ethical and societal repercussions.

Basic Principles of Vegetarian Cooking

At its core, vegetarian cooking revolves around the exclusion of animal products, relying instead on a diverse array of fruits, vegetables, grains, legumes, nuts, seeds, and dairy or plant-based alternatives. From these foundational elements, several basic principles emerge, shaping the essence of vegetarian cuisine.

Foundation of Ingredients

- Plant Diversity: Vegetarian cooking thrives on the diversity of plant-based ingredients. This includes a rainbow of vegetables, from leafy greens like kale and spinach to root vegetables like carrots and beets, providing a spectrum of flavors, textures, and nutrients.

- Grains and Legumes: Staples like quinoa, brown rice, lentils, and beans serve as substantial sources of protein and carbohydrates in vegetarian diets. Their versatility allows for a wide range of dishes, from hearty stews to flavorful salads.

- Nuts, Seeds, and Oils: These ingredients add richness and depth to vegetarian dishes. Nuts like almonds, walnuts, and cashews offer texture and healthy fats, while seeds such as chia, flax, and sesame provide crunch and nutritional benefits. Various oils like olive, coconut, and avocado contribute distinct flavors and are used for cooking and dressing.

Flavor Enhancement

- Herbs and Spices: The use of herbs and spices elevates vegetarian dishes, offering complexity and depth of flavor without relying on meat. Cumin, paprika, turmeric, coriander, and cinnamon are just a few examples that lend distinctive tastes to dishes.

- Umami Components: Ingredients like mushrooms, nutritional yeast, soy sauce, miso, and tamari add umami, the savory fifth taste, enhancing the overall depth and richness of vegetarian cooking.

- Acid Balance: Incorporating acids like citrus juices, vinegar, or tomatoes helps balance flavors, cutting through richness and adding brightness to dishes.

Cooking Techniques

- Sautéing and Stir-Frying: These quick-cooking methods preserve the texture and nutrients of vegetables while adding a caramelized depth of flavor.

- Roasting and Grilling: These techniques intensify the natural sweetness of vegetables, lending them a smoky or caramelized taste that enhances their appeal.

- Steaming and Boiling: Ideal for retaining the nutritional value of vegetables, especially delicate ones, without adding excess fats.

Balance and Nutrition

- Protein Sources: Vegetarian cooking requires careful consideration to ensure adequate protein intake. Combining grains and legumes or incorporating tofu, tempeh, seitan, or plant-based meat substitutes can provide a complete protein profile.

- Balanced Meals: Creating well-rounded meals involves incorporating a variety of nutrients—carbohydrates, proteins, healthy fats, vitamins, and minerals—through diverse ingredients.

- Whole Foods Emphasis: Emphasizing whole, unprocessed foods ensures the intake of essential nutrients while minimizing reliance on processed vegetarian alternatives, which may contain additives and preservatives.

Creativity and Adaptability

- Recipe Adaptation: Vegetarian cooking invites creativity and adaptability. Traditional recipes can often be modified or reimagined by substituting meat with plant-based alternatives or enhancing flavors through innovative ingredient combinations.

- Cultural Influences: Drawing inspiration from various culinary traditions worldwide allows for a diverse and exciting array of vegetarian dishes, from Indian curries to Mediterranean mezze spreads.

- Experimentation: Exploring new ingredients, flavor pairings, and cooking techniques fosters culinary growth and keeps vegetarian cooking fresh and exciting.

Mindful Cooking and Sustainability

- Local and Seasonal Produce: Prioritizing locally sourced and seasonal produce supports sustainability efforts while ensuring freshness and optimal flavor in dishes.

- Reducing Food Waste: Utilizing parts of vegetables that are often discarded, such as carrot tops or broccoli stalks, reduces waste and expands the repertoire of dishes.

- Mindful Consumption: Consciousness about food choices and their environmental impact encourages responsible consumption and appreciation for the origins of ingredients.

The principles of vegetarian cooking embody a harmonious blend of ingredient diversity, flavor enhancement, versatile cooking techniques, nutritional balance, creativity, adaptability, and mindful practices. Embracing these principles not only leads to delicious and nourishing meals but also fosters a deeper connection to food, health, and the environment.

Essential ingredients

The vegetarian diet, rich in plant-based foods, is characterized by its diversity and nutrient density. Its foundation rests on a wide array of essential ingredients that provide not only sustenance but also an abundance of flavors and health benefits. From fruits and vegetables to legumes, grains, nuts, and seeds, these components form the bedrock of a nutritious and vibrant vegetarian diet.

Fruits and Vegetables

- Leafy Greens: Kale, spinach, Swiss chard, and collard greens are nutrient powerhouses, packed with vitamins A, C, K, and folate. They serve as versatile ingredients in salads, smoothies, stir-fries, and soups.

- Colorful Vegetables: Bell peppers, tomatoes, carrots, beets, and eggplants offer a spectrum of antioxidants, phytonutrients, and fiber, contributing to overall health and disease prevention.

- Cruciferous Vegetables: Broccoli, cauliflower, Brussels sprouts, and cabbage contain compounds linked to cancer prevention and are excellent sources of vitamins, minerals, and fiber.

- Root Vegetables: Potatoes, sweet potatoes, carrots, and turnips are hearty and versatile, providing complex carbohydrates, fiber, and an array of vitamins and minerals.

- Fruits: Berries, citrus fruits, apples, bananas, and tropical fruits like mangoes and papayas offer a sweet and nutritious addition to the diet, providing vitamins, antioxidants, and dietary fiber.

Grains and Legumes

- Whole Grains: Quinoa, brown rice, bulgur, oats, and barley are rich in fiber, B vitamins, and minerals like iron and magnesium, offering sustained energy and aiding in digestive health.

- Legumes: Lentils, chickpeas, black beans, and kidney beans are protein powerhouses, packed with fiber, iron, and essential minerals, making them an integral part of vegetarian meals.

- Soy Products: Tofu, tempeh, and edamame are versatile soy-based ingredients providing complete protein, essential amino acids, and calcium, commonly used in various vegetarian dishes.

Nuts and Seeds

- Almonds: Rich in healthy fats, protein, fiber, and vitamin E, almonds contribute to heart health and provide a satisfying crunch to dishes or serve as a base for creamy sauces.

- Walnuts: These nuts contain omega-3 fatty acids, promoting brain health and reducing inflammation. They add a nutty flavor to salads, baked goods, or as a topping for oatmeal or yogurt.

- Chia Seeds: High in fiber, omega-3 fatty acids, and antioxidants, chia seeds are a versatile addition to smoothies, puddings, or as a binding agent in vegan baking.

- Flaxseeds: Another source of omega-3 fatty acids, flaxseeds offer a nutty flavor and are commonly ground and added to smoothies, oatmeal, or baked goods for a nutritional boost.

Dairy and Plant-Based Alternatives

- Milk Alternatives: Soy, almond, oat, coconut, and rice milk are popular plant-based alternatives rich in vitamins and minerals, suitable for drinking, baking, or cooking.

- Yogurt Alternatives: Plant-based yogurts made from coconut, almond, or soy provide probiotics and can be used in both sweet and savory dishes.

- Cheese Alternatives: Nutritional yeast, tofu-based cheeses, and cashew-based spreads offer alternatives to traditional dairy cheese, adding flavor and texture to dishes.

Healthy Fats and Oils

- Olive Oil: A staple in Mediterranean cuisine, olive oil contains monounsaturated fats and antioxidants, used in dressings, sautéing, and roasting.

- Coconut Oil: Known for its medium-chain triglycerides (MCTs), coconut oil is popular in vegan baking and cooking, and as a flavorful addition to dishes.

- Avocado: High in healthy fats and potassium, avocados add creaminess to dishes like salads, and sandwiches, or as a topping for toast.

Herbs, Spices, and Condiments

- Herbs: Basil, cilantro, parsley, thyme, and rosemary add depth and flavor to vegetarian dishes, enhancing their aromatic profiles.

- Spices: Cumin, turmeric, paprika, cinnamon, and chili powder contribute not only to taste but also offer numerous health benefits due to their antioxidant and anti-inflammatory properties.
- Condiments: Tamari, soy sauce, miso, tahini, and nutritional yeast are flavorful additions used to elevate the taste of various vegetarian dishes.

Importance of Balance and Diversity

While these ingredients form the essential components of a vegetarian diet, balance and diversity are crucial. Combining different food groups ensures the intake of essential nutrients such as protein, iron, calcium, vitamin B12, and omega-3 fatty acids. Incorporating a wide variety of these ingredients not only enhances the culinary experience but also promotes overall health and well-being.

Kitchen tools and equipment

Whether you're a seasoned chef or a novice cook, having the right tools can significantly simplify the process and elevate your vegetarian cooking experience. From basic utensils to specialized appliances, these kitchen tools and equipment are indispensable for creating delicious vegetarian dishes.

Essential Utensils

- Chef's Knife: A high-quality chef's knife is a kitchen staple, indispensable for chopping vegetables, fruits, and herbs with precision and ease.

- Cutting Boards: Having multiple cutting boards—one for vegetables, another for fruits, and a separate one for cooked foods—prevents cross-contamination and ensures food safety.

- Vegetable Peeler: A reliable vegetable peeler simplifies the task of peeling potatoes, carrots, and other root vegetables, saving time and effort.

- Mixing Bowls: A set of mixing bowls in various sizes is essential for combining ingredients, tossing salads, and preparing dressings or marinades.

- Colander/Strainer: Ideal for rinsing grains, legumes, and vegetables or draining pasta, a colander or strainer is a versatile tool in vegetarian cooking.

- Measuring Cups and Spoons: Accurate measurements are crucial in baking or following recipes, making these essential for precise ingredient quantities.

- Kitchen Scale: For those who prefer precise measurements, a kitchen scale is invaluable for portioning ingredients accurately.

Cooking Tools

- Non-Stick Cookware: A good quality non-stick skillet or frying pan prevents food from sticking and requires less oil, perfect for sautéing vegetables or making pancakes and omelets.

- Saucepan and Stockpot: Essential for cooking grains, legumes, soups, stews, and sauces, these versatile pots are a kitchen necessity.

- Baking Sheets: Used for roasting vegetables, baking cookies, or making homemade granola, baking sheets with rims prevent spillage and ease food transfer.

- Blender or Food Processor: These appliances are versatile for creating soups, sauces, smoothies, nut butters, and finely chopping vegetables or nuts.

- Immersion Blender: Ideal for blending soups directly in the pot and creating creamy textures without transferring hot liquids to a blender.

- Grater/Zester: Essential for grating cheese, zesting citrus fruits, or shredding vegetables like carrots and zucchini for salads or baking.
- Vegetable Spiralizer: For creating vegetable noodles from zucchini, carrots, or beets, adding variety and creativity to vegetarian meals.

Specialized Appliances

- Slow Cooker or Crock-Pot: Perfect for preparing soups, stews, and bean-based dishes with minimal effort, allowing flavors to meld over time.
- Rice Cooker: Simplifies the cooking process for various grains like rice, quinoa, or barley, ensuring consistent results every time.

- Pressure Cooker/Instant Pot: A multi-functional appliance that speeds up cooking times for grains, legumes, and beans, offering convenience without compromising flavor.

- Dehydrator: For drying fruits, making vegetable chips, or creating homemade dried herbs, adding variety and preserving seasonal produce.

- Juicer: Ideal for extracting fresh juices from fruits and vegetables, offering a nutrient-rich beverage option.

Accessories and Miscellaneous Items

- Tongs and Spatulas: Useful for flipping vegetables, stirring sauces, or handling delicate foods without damaging them.

- Kitchen Shears: Multipurpose scissors for cutting herbs, trimming vegetables, or even spatchcocking vegetables for roasting.

- Silicone Spatulas and Whisks: Versatile tools for mixing, stirring, scraping bowls, and folding ingredients together.

- Kitchen Towels and Oven Mitts: Essential for handling hot cookware, drying hands, and wiping countertops during cooking.

- Storage Containers: Having a variety of containers for storing leftovers, prepped ingredients, or packed lunches promotes organization and reduces food waste.

Importance of Quality and Maintenance

Investing in high-quality kitchen tools and equipment can enhance the cooking experience, offering durability, efficiency, and better results in food preparation. Regular maintenance, including proper cleaning and storage, ensures longevity and optimal performance of these tools.

Tips for meal planning

Meal planning is a key element in successfully maintaining a nutritious and satisfying vegetarian diet. It not only streamlines the cooking process but also ensures a well-balanced intake of essential nutrients. Here are some tips for effective meal planning in a vegetarian diet:

1. Embrace Variety and Balance

- Include Various Food Groups: Ensure meals contain a mix of vegetables, fruits, whole grains, legumes, nuts, seeds, and dairy or plant-based alternatives to meet diverse nutritional needs.
- Rotate Ingredients: Incorporate a variety of vegetables, grains, and legumes throughout the week to ensure a wide range of nutrients and prevent monotony.
- Consider Protein Sources: Focus on incorporating diverse protein sources such as tofu, tempeh, lentils, chickpeas, quinoa, and beans to fulfill protein requirements.

2. Plan Ahead

- Set Aside Time for Planning: Dedicate a specific time each week to plan meals, create shopping lists, and prep ingredients in advance to streamline cooking during busy days.

- Use Meal Planning Tools: Utilize apps, meal planning templates, or calendars to organize meal ideas, recipes, and grocery lists for the week.

- Batch Cooking and Prep: Prepare larger quantities of grains, beans, or roasted vegetables that can be used in multiple meals throughout the week for quick assembly.

3. Create Balanced Meals

- Plan Balanced Meals: Aim for meals that include a source of protein, healthy fats, complex carbohydrates, and a variety of vegetables or fruits to create satisfying and nutritious dishes.

- Mix Up Cooking Techniques: Incorporate different cooking methods like roasting, steaming, sautéing, or grilling to add variety and depth of flavors to meals.

- Consider Meal Components: Plan meals with a main dish (grains or protein source), complemented by sides (vegetables, salads, or soups) for a well-rounded plate.

4. Utilize Leftovers and Repurpose Ingredients

- Plan for Leftovers: Prepare larger batches of meals or ingredients to use leftovers for subsequent meals, reducing cooking time on busy days.

- Repurpose Ingredients: Transform leftover grains or vegetables into new dishes like stir-fries, salads, soups, or grain bowls to minimize food waste.

- Make Ingredient Substitutions: Use versatile ingredients that can be repurposed in multiple dishes, such as cooked quinoa for salads, stuffed peppers, or as a base for patties.

5. Seasonal and Local Eating

- Incorporate Seasonal Produce: Plan meals around seasonal fruits and vegetables for optimal flavor, freshness, and cost-effectiveness.

- Support Local Markets: Explore local farmer's markets or community-supported agriculture (CSA) programs to access fresh, locally grown produce, enhancing meal variety and supporting local farmers.

- Plan Around Special Occasions or Events: Adjust meal plans to accommodate special occasions or events, incorporating celebratory dishes while maintaining a balanced diet.

6. Flexibility and Experimentation

- Be Flexible: Allow for flexibility in meal planning to accommodate changes in schedule, unexpected events, or last-minute cravings.

- Experiment with New Recipes: Incorporate new vegetarian recipes or try different cuisines to keep meals exciting and expand culinary horizons.

- Plan Theme Nights: Designate specific days for different cuisine themes (Mexican, Italian, Asian) to add variety and excitement to meals throughout the week.

7. Mindful Eating and Portion Control

- Mindful Portioning: Pay attention to portion sizes to ensure a balanced intake of nutrients while preventing overeating or food wastage.
- Focus on Whole Foods: Prioritize whole, minimally processed foods over highly processed vegetarian alternatives for better nutritional value.

- Listen to Your Body: Be attentive to hunger cues and nutritional needs, adjusting meal plans accordingly to meet individual dietary requirements.

Chapter 2

Essential Cooking Techniques

Knife Skills and Cutting Techniques

Knife skills are crucial for anyone following a vegetarian diet. With a focus on fresh produce, mastering various cutting techniques not only enhances the aesthetics of dishes but also impacts their texture and flavor. Here are some essential cutting techniques and their applications in a vegetarian diet:

- Julienne: Cutting vegetables into thin, uniform matchsticks. Ideal for stir-fries, salads, and garnishes. Vegetables like carrots, bell peppers, and zucchinis work well.

- Dice: Creating uniform cubes of vegetables. Useful for soups, stews, and sautés. Potatoes, onions, and tomatoes are commonly diced.

- Chiffonade: Rolling leafy greens into a tight cylinder and slicing thinly. Perfect for adding ribbons of greens to salads, soups, or garnishing dishes with basil or mint.

- Brunoise: A finer dice than regular cubes, used for flavor bases like mirepoix (onions, carrots, and celery) in stocks, sauces, and soups.

- Mincing: Cutting ingredients into tiny pieces. Garlic, ginger, and herbs are often minced to infuse flavor throughout a dish.
- Slicing: Cutting vegetables or fruits into even slices. This technique works for tomatoes, cucumbers, and eggplants, among others, for layering in casseroles or making veggie chips.
- Ripping/Tearing: For herbs and salad greens, tearing them gently by hand helps retain their natural textures and flavors.

Proper knife handling and safety are as important as the techniques themselves. Always use a sharp knife to prevent accidents, and maintain a stable cutting surface.

When preparing a vegetarian diet, these skills ensure vegetables are cut appropriately for different cooking methods—whether it's a stir-fry, a roasted medley, or a fresh salad. Uniform cuts help in even cooking, while varied cuts add visual appeal and texture to meals.

Sauteing, roasting, steaming, and grilling

1. Sauteing

This quick cooking method involves cooking vegetables over medium-high heat in a small amount of oil or butter. It's great for tender vegetables like bell peppers, zucchini, or mushrooms. The high heat caramelizes the natural sugars, imparting a rich flavor and maintaining some crunch. To prevent overcrowding the pan, which leads to steaming instead of sauteing, ensure the vegetables have enough space to brown evenly.

2. Roasting

One of the best methods for intensifying flavors, roasting involves cooking vegetables in the oven at high temperatures. It works wonderfully with root vegetables such as carrots, potatoes, and beets, as well as with cauliflower, broccoli, and Brussels sprouts. Tossing veggies in olive oil, salt, and spices before roasting caramelizes their sugars, resulting in a deliciously crispy exterior and a tender interior.

3. Steaming

A gentle and healthy cooking method that retains the vegetables' nutrients, colors, and textures. Steaming is perfect for more delicate vegetables like broccoli, asparagus, and green beans. It involves cooking the vegetables over boiling water in a steamer basket or covered pot. Be mindful of not overcooking them to maintain their vibrant colors and crispness.

4. Grilling

This method adds a smoky flavor to vegetables and creates beautiful grill marks. It's fantastic for heartier veggies like eggplant, bell peppers, and corn on the cob. Brushing the vegetables with oil and seasoning them before grilling helps prevent sticking and adds flavor. Grilling also allows for creativity by infusing veggies with a smoky taste that pairs well with various marinades or sauces.

Each of these methods offers different textures and flavors, allowing you to create diverse dishes even with the same vegetables. For example, a medley of roasted vegetables can be a side dish, tossed in pasta, or used in wraps or sandwiches, showcasing their versatility.

Experimenting with seasonings, herbs, and spices can elevate the flavors further. For instance, adding garlic and thyme while roasting carrots or using a soy sauce-based marinade for grilled eggplant can completely transform the taste profile.

How to properly cook various vegetables

Properly cooking vegetables is key to bringing out their flavors, textures, and maximizing their nutritional value. Here's a breakdown of how to cook various vegetables:

1. Leafy Greens (Spinach, Kale, Swiss Chard)

Sauteing or Steaming: Cook until wilted but still vibrant. Adding garlic, lemon juice, or a splash of vinegar can enhance their taste.

2. Root Vegetables (Carrots, Potatoes, Beets)

Roasting or Steaming: Roasting brings out their natural sweetness, while steaming retains their nutrients. Cut them uniformly for even cooking.

3. Cruciferous Vegetables (Broccoli, Cauliflower, Brussels Sprouts)

Roasting or Steaming: Roasting caramelizes their natural sugars, making them crispy outside and tender inside. Steaming retains their texture and nutrients.

4. Alliums (Onions, Garlic, Leeks)

Sauteing or Roasting: Saute onions until translucent to release their sweetness. Roasting garlic cloves brings a mild, nutty flavor.

5. Nightshades (Tomatoes, Eggplant, Peppers)

Grilling or Roasting: Grilling adds a smoky flavor to eggplant and peppers, while roasting concentrates the sweetness of tomatoes.

6. Mushrooms

Sauteing or Roasting: Saute mushrooms until golden brown to enhance their umami flavor. Roasting intensifies their taste and creates a meatier texture.

7. Squash and Zucchini

Roasting or Grilling: Both methods caramelize the natural sugars, bringing out a rich flavor. Thin slices work well for grilling, while cubes are great for roasting.

8. Corn

Grilling or Boiling: Grilling corn adds a smoky flavor, while boiling keeps it crisp and sweet. Husks can be removed before grilling or kept on for boiling.

9. Green Beans and Asparagus

Steaming or Sauteing: Steaming retains their bright color and crispness, while sauteing with garlic or lemon zest adds flavor.

10. Peas and Carrots

Steaming or Stir-Frying: Steam for a short time to keep them crisp or stir-fry with other vegetables to infuse flavors. Cooking times can vary based on the size and type of vegetable, so it's essential to monitor them while cooking and avoid overcooking, which can lead to mushiness and loss of nutrients.

Chapter 3

Building Blocks of Flavor

Understanding Herbs, Spices, and Seasonings

Understanding Herbs, Spices, and Seasonings is essential for mastering the art of vegetarian cooking. Herbs are derived from the leaves of plants, while spices are usually obtained from seeds, bark, roots, or fruits of plants. Both impart unique flavors, aromas, and health benefits to dishes.

Commonly used herbs in vegetarian cooking include basil, cilantro, parsley, thyme, and rosemary. Each herb carries distinct flavor profiles; for instance, basil offers a sweet, peppery taste, while cilantro contributes a fresh, citrus-like flavor. These herbs can elevate the taste of dishes when used fresh or dried.

Spices play a pivotal role in adding depth and complexity to vegetarian meals. Some popular spices include cumin, coriander, turmeric, paprika, and cinnamon. Cumin brings a warm, earthy flavor, while turmeric provides a vibrant yellow hue and a slightly bitter taste. Understanding how to balance these spices is key to creating harmonious flavor profiles in vegetarian dishes.

Combining herbs and spices strategically can enhance the overall taste of a dish. For instance, pairing basil and oregano can create an Italian-inspired flavor, while combining cumin and coriander can offer a depth of warmth in Indian cuisine. Understanding these flavor profiles empowers individuals to experiment and create unique blends that suit their preferences.

Moving on to Homemade Sauces and Dressings, these versatile additions can elevate the simplest of vegetarian meals. Making sauces and dressings from scratch allows for customization and ensures the use of fresh, wholesome ingredients.

One simple yet versatile sauce is a classic tomato marinara. Combining tomatoes, garlic, basil, and oregano cooked gently with olive oil results in a flavorful sauce that can accompany pasta, and vegetables, or be used as a pizza base.

Another option is a tahini dressing made from tahini paste, lemon juice, garlic, and water. This creamy, tangy dressing adds depth to salads, and roasted vegetables, or can be used as a dip.

Experimenting with different ingredients and ratios is key to creating personalized sauces and dressings that cater to individual taste preferences.

When it comes to Simple Recipes for Versatile Sauces and Dressings, there are numerous options. One example is a basic vinaigrette made by combining olive oil, balsamic vinegar, Dijon mustard, honey, salt, and pepper. This dressing can be modified by adding herbs like thyme or rosemary for added depth.

Another simple sauce is a pesto made from fresh basil, pine nuts, garlic, Parmesan cheese, and olive oil. It can be used as a pasta sauce, spread on sandwiches, or even as a topping for grilled vegetables.

Understanding the basics of these sauces and dressings serves as a foundation for improvisation and innovation in the kitchen. It allows individuals to tailor flavors according to their preferences while ensuring the use of wholesome ingredients.

Mastering the use of herbs, spices, and seasonings in vegetarian cooking opens up a world of flavors and possibilities. Pairing different herbs and spices, creating homemade sauces and dressings, and experimenting with simple yet versatile recipes can transform ordinary vegetarian dishes into culinary delights. It's not just about following recipes but understanding the fundamentals of flavor profiles and how they complement each other, giving individuals the confidence to explore their creativity in the kitchen.

Chapter 4

Breakfast and Brunch Delights

Avocado Toast

Preparation time: 5 minutes

Cooking time: 5 minutes

Number of servings: 2

Ingredients:

- 2 ripe avocados

- 4 slices of whole-grain bread

- 1 tablespoon olive oil

- Salt and pepper to taste
- Optional toppings: red pepper flakes, sliced tomatoes, feta cheese, etc.

Directions:

1. Cut the avocados in half, remove the pit, and scoop out the flesh into a bowl.
2. Mash the avocado with a fork until it reaches your desired consistency. Add salt and pepper to taste.
3. Toast the slices of bread until golden brown.
4. Drizzle olive oil over the toast.
5. Spread the mashed avocado evenly on the toast.
6. Add optional toppings as desired.
7. Serve immediately and enjoy!

Nutritional info: (per serving, without optional toppings)

- Calories: 250
- Total Fat: 15g
- Saturated Fat: 2g
- Carbohydrates: 25g
- Fiber: 8g
- Protein: 5g

Vegetable Omelette

Preparation time: 10 minutes

Cooking time: 10 minutes

Number of servings: 2

Ingredients:

- 4 eggs

- 1/4 cup chopped bell peppers

- 1/4 cup chopped onions

- 1/4 cup chopped tomatoes

- 1/4 cup chopped spinach

- 1/4 cup shredded cheese (optional)

- Salt and pepper to taste

- 1 tablespoon olive oil

Directions:

1. Crack the eggs into a bowl, season with salt and pepper, and whisk until well combined.

2. Heat olive oil in a non-stick skillet over medium heat.

3. Add chopped vegetables to the skillet and sauté until they soften, about 3-4 minutes.

4. Pour the beaten eggs over the vegetables evenly.
5. Let the omelette cook undisturbed for 2-3 minutes until the edges start to set.
6. Sprinkle shredded cheese (if using) over half of the omelette.
7. Gently fold the omelette in half using a spatula.
8. Cook for another 2 minutes until the cheese melts and the eggs are fully cooked.
9. Slide the omelette onto a plate, slice, and serve hot.

Nutritional info: (per serving, without cheese)

- Calories: 180
- Total Fat: 12g
- Saturated Fat: 3g

- Carbohydrates: 5g
- Fiber: 1g
- Protein: 13g

Blueberry Pancakes

Preparation time: 10 minutes

Cooking time: 15 minutes

Number of servings: 4

Ingredients:

- 1 cup all-purpose flour
- 2 tablespoons sugar
- 1 teaspoon baking powder
- 1/2 teaspoon baking soda
- 1/4 teaspoon salt

- 1 cup buttermilk
- 1 large egg
- 2 tablespoons melted butter
- 1 cup fresh or frozen blueberries
- Butter or oil for cooking

Directions:

1. In a mixing bowl, whisk together flour, sugar, baking powder, baking soda, and salt.
2. In another bowl, whisk buttermilk, egg, and melted butter until well combined.
3. Pour the wet ingredients into the dry ingredients and mix until just combined. Don't overmix; lumps are okay.
4. Gently fold in the blueberries.

5. Heat a skillet or griddle over medium heat and grease lightly with butter or oil.
6. Pour 1/4 cup of batter onto the skillet for each pancake.
7. Cook until bubbles form on the surface, then flip and cook the other side until golden brown.
8. Repeat with the remaining batter.
9. Serve the pancakes warm with maple syrup or toppings of your choice.

    Nutritional info: (per serving, without toppings)

- Calories: 250
- Total Fat: 7g
- Saturated Fat: 4g

- Carbohydrates: 40g

- Fiber: 2g

- Protein: 6g

Greek Yogurt Parfait

Preparation time: 5 minutes

Number of servings: 2

Ingredients:

- 1 cup Greek yogurt

- 1/2 cup granola

- 1 cup mixed berries (strawberries, blueberries, raspberries)

- Honey or maple syrup (optional)

- Nuts or seeds for topping (optional)

Directions:

1. In two glasses or bowls, start layering the ingredients. Begin with a spoonful of Greek yogurt at the bottom.
2. Add a layer of granola on top of the yogurt.
3. Follow with a layer of mixed berries.
4. Repeat the layers until the glass or bowl is filled, ending with a final layer of berries.
5. Drizzle honey or maple syrup over the top if desired.
6. Sprinkle nuts or seeds on top for an extra crunch.
7. Serve immediately and enjoy your refreshing parfait!

Nutritional info: (per serving)

- Calories: 250
- Total Fat: 6g
- Saturated Fat: 1g
- Carbohydrates: 35g
- Fiber: 5g
- Protein: 15g

Veggie Breakfast Burrito

Preparation time: 15 minutes

Cooking time: 10 minutes

Number of servings: 2

Ingredients:

- 4 large eggs
- 1/4 cup diced bell peppers

- 1/4 cup diced onions

- 1/4 cup diced tomatoes

- 1/2 cup chopped spinach

- 1/2 cup shredded cheese

- 2 large flour tortillas

- Salt and pepper to taste

- Salsa or hot sauce (optional)

Directions:

1. In a bowl, beat the eggs and season with salt and pepper.

2. Heat a skillet over medium heat and add a bit of oil.

3. Sauté bell peppers, onions, and tomatoes until softened, about 3-4 minutes.

4. Add chopped spinach to the skillet and cook for an additional 1-2 minutes until wilted.

5. Pour the beaten eggs into the skillet with the vegetables and scramble until cooked through.

6. Warm the tortillas in the microwave or on a separate skillet.

7. Divide the scrambled eggs mixture between the tortillas.

8. Sprinkle shredded cheese on top of the eggs.

9. Roll the tortillas, folding in the sides to enclose the filling.

10. Optionally, heat the burritos in a skillet for a minute on each side until golden.

11. Serve with salsa or hot sauce if desired.

Nutritional info: (per serving)

- Calories: 400

- Total Fat: 20g
- Saturated Fat: 8g
- Carbohydrates: 30g
- Fiber: 4g
- Protein: 25g

Spinach and Feta Quiche

Preparation time: 15 minutes

Cooking time: 45 minutes

Number of servings: 6

Ingredients:

- 1 pie crust (store-bought or homemade)
- 6 large eggs
- 1 cup milk or heavy cream

- 2 cups fresh spinach, chopped
- 1 cup crumbled feta cheese
- 1/2 cup diced onions
- Salt and pepper to taste
- Pinch of nutmeg (optional)

Directions:

1. Preheat the oven to 375°F (190°C).
2. Place the pie crust in a pie dish and crimp the edges.
3. In a bowl, whisk together eggs, milk (or cream), salt, pepper, and nutmeg if using.
4. Spread chopped spinach, feta cheese, and diced onions evenly over the pie crust.
5. Pour the egg mixture over the spinach and feta.

6. Place the quiche in the oven and bake for 40-45 minutes or until the center is set and the crust is golden brown.
7. Remove from the oven and let it cool for a few minutes before slicing.
8. Serve warm or at room temperature.

Nutritional info: (per serving)

- Calories: 320
- Total Fat: 21g
- Saturated Fat: 10g
- Carbohydrates: 20g
- Fiber: 1g
- Protein: 15g

Banana Walnut Muffins

Preparation time: 15 minutes

Cooking time: 20 minutes

Number of servings: 12

Ingredients:

- 2 cups all-purpose flour
- 1 teaspoon baking powder
- 1 teaspoon baking soda
- 1/2 teaspoon salt
- 3 ripe bananas, mashed
- 1/2 cup granulated sugar
- 1/2 cup unsalted butter, melted
- 2 large eggs
- 1 teaspoon vanilla extract
- 1/2 cup chopped walnuts

Directions:

1. Preheat the oven to 375°F (190°C). Line a muffin tin with paper liners or grease the cups.
2. In a bowl, whisk together the flour, baking powder, baking soda, and salt.
3. In another bowl, mix together mashed bananas, sugar, melted butter, eggs, and vanilla extract until well combined.
4. Gradually add the dry ingredients into the wet ingredients and mix until just combined. Do not overmix.
5. Gently fold in the chopped walnuts.
6. Spoon the batter into the prepared muffin cups, filling each about two-thirds full.

7. Bake for 18-20 minutes or until a toothpick inserted into the center of a muffin comes out clean.

8. Remove the muffins from the oven and let them cool in the pan for 5 minutes before transferring to a wire rack to cool completely.

Nutritional info: (per muffin)

- Calories: 220
- Total Fat: 10g
- Saturated Fat: 4g
- Carbohydrates: 30g
- Fiber: 2g
- Protein: 4g

Tofu Scramble

Preparation time: 10 minutes

Cooking time: 10 minutes

Number of servings: 2

Ingredients:

- 1 block firm tofu, drained and crumbled
- 1 tablespoon olive oil
- 1/2 cup diced bell peppers
- 1/4 cup diced onions
- 1/2 cup chopped spinach
- 1 teaspoon turmeric powder
- 1/2 teaspoon garlic powder
- Salt and pepper to taste
- Optional: nutritional yeast, chopped tomatoes, avocado slices

Directions:

1. Heat olive oil in a skillet over medium heat.
2. Add diced bell peppers and onions to the skillet and sauté for 2-3 minutes until they begin to soften.
3. Add crumbled tofu to the skillet and stir well.
4. Sprinkle turmeric powder and garlic powder over the tofu and mix until the tofu is evenly coated.
5. Add chopped spinach to the skillet and continue cooking for another 2-3 minutes until the spinach wilts.
6. Season with salt and pepper to taste.
7. Optionally, sprinkle nutritional yeast over the tofu scramble for a cheesy flavor.

8. Serve the tofu scramble hot with chopped tomatoes or avocado slices if desired.

Nutritional info: (per serving)

- Calories: 220
- Total Fat: 14g
- Saturated Fat: 2g
- Carbohydrates: 8g
- Fiber: 3g
- Protein: 18g

Chia Seed Pudding

Preparation time: 5 minutes (plus chilling time)

Number of servings: 2

Ingredients:

- 1/4 cup chia seeds

- 1 cup almond milk or any milk of choice

- 1 tablespoon maple syrup or honey

- 1/2 teaspoon vanilla extract

- Fresh fruits, nuts, or seeds for topping (optional)

Directions:

1. In a bowl or jar, mix together chia seeds, almond milk, maple syrup (or honey), and vanilla extract.
2. Stir well to combine, making sure there are no clumps of chia seeds.
3. Cover the bowl or jar and refrigerate for at least 2 hours or overnight, allowing the mixture to thicken.

4. After chilling, give the pudding a stir as the chia seeds tend to settle at the bottom.
5. Serve the chia seed pudding in bowls or jars and top with fresh fruits, nuts, or seeds if desired.

Nutritional info: (per serving)

- Calories: 150
- Total Fat: 7g
- Saturated Fat: 1g
- Carbohydrates: 18g
- Fiber: 9g
- Protein: 5g

Breakfast Quesadilla

Preparation time: 10 minutes

Cooking time: 10 minutes

Number of servings: 2

Ingredients:

- 4 large flour tortillas
- 4 large eggs
- 1/2 cup shredded cheese (cheddar, Monterey Jack, or your choice)
- 1/4 cup diced bell peppers
- 1/4 cup diced onions
- 1/2 cup cooked and crumbled breakfast sausage or diced ham (optional)
- Salt and pepper to taste
- Salsa, sour cream, or guacamole for serving (optional)

Directions:

1. In a bowl, whisk the eggs and season with salt and pepper.
2. Heat a skillet over medium heat and lightly grease it with oil or butter.
3. Pour the beaten eggs into the skillet and scramble them until cooked through.
4. Remove the scrambled eggs from the skillet and set them aside.
5. On a clean skillet or griddle, place a tortilla.
6. Sprinkle a layer of shredded cheese over half of the tortilla.
7. Add a portion of scrambled eggs, diced bell peppers, onions, and cooked sausage or ham (if using) on top of the cheese.
8. Fold the tortilla in half, covering the filling.

9. Press the quesadilla gently and cook for 2-3 minutes on each side until golden and the cheese melts.//
10. Repeat the process with the remaining tortillas and filling ingredients.
11. Cut the quesadillas into wedges and serve with salsa, sour cream, or guacamole if desired.

    Nutritional info: (per serving, without optional toppings)

- Calories: 380
- Total Fat: 20g
- Saturated Fat: 8g
- Carbohydrates: 28g
- Fiber: 2g
- Protein: 20g

Mixed Berry Smoothie Bowl

Preparation time: 5 minutes

Number of servings: 2

Ingredients:

- 2 ripe bananas, sliced and frozen
- 1 cup mixed berries (strawberries, blueberries, raspberries)
- 1/2 cup plain Greek yogurt
- 1/4 cup almond milk or any milk of choice
- Toppings: sliced fruits, granola, shredded coconut, chia seeds, etc.

Directions:

1. In a blender, combine frozen banana slices, mixed berries, Greek yogurt, and almond milk.
2. Blend until smooth and creamy, adding more milk if needed to reach the desired consistency.
3. Pour the smoothie into bowls.
4. Top the smoothie bowls with sliced fruits, granola, shredded coconut, chia seeds, or any toppings of your choice.

Nutritional info: (per serving, without toppings)

- Calories: 180
- Total Fat: 2g
- Saturated Fat: 0g
- Carbohydrates: 35g
- Fiber: 5g

- Protein: 8g

Veggie Hash Browns

Preparation time: 15 minutes

Cooking time: 15 minutes

Number of servings: 4

Ingredients:

- 4 cups grated potatoes (about 2 large potatoes)
- 1/2 cup grated carrots
- 1/4 cup finely chopped onions
- 1/4 cup finely chopped bell peppers
- 2 tablespoons all-purpose flour or cornstarch
- 1 teaspoon garlic powder
- 1 teaspoon paprika

- Salt and pepper to taste
- Cooking oil

Directions:

1. In a bowl, combine grated potatoes, grated carrots, chopped onions, chopped bell peppers, flour or cornstarch, garlic powder, paprika, salt, and pepper.
2. Heat a skillet or griddle over medium-high heat and add enough oil to coat the surface.
3. Take a portion of the potato mixture and shape it into a patty, pressing it firmly together.
4. Place the patties on the hot skillet and cook for 5-7 minutes on each side, or until golden brown and crispy.

5. Remove the hash browns from the skillet and place them on a paper towel-lined plate to absorb excess oil.
6. Repeat the process with the remaining potato mixture, adding more oil to the skillet as needed.
7. Serve the veggie hash browns hot as a delicious breakfast side.

Nutritional info: (per serving)

- Calories: 160
- Total Fat: 3g
- Saturated Fat: 0g
- Carbohydrates: 30g
- Fiber: 3g
- Protein: 3g

Mushroom and Spinach Frittata

Preparation time: 10 minutes

Cooking time: 20 minutes

Number of servings: 4

Ingredients:

- 8 large eggs
- 1 cup sliced mushrooms
- 2 cups fresh spinach
- 1/2 cup diced onions
- 1/2 cup shredded cheese (cheddar, mozzarella, or your choice)
- 2 tablespoons olive oil
- Salt and pepper to taste

Directions:

1. Preheat the oven to 350°F (175°C).
2. In a bowl, whisk the eggs and season with salt and pepper.
3. Heat olive oil in an oven-safe skillet over medium heat.
4. Sauté the diced onions until translucent, then add the sliced mushrooms and cook until they soften.
5. Add fresh spinach to the skillet and cook until wilted.
6. Spread the vegetables evenly in the skillet.
7. Pour the whisked eggs over the vegetables.
8. Cook on the stovetop for about 3-4 minutes until the edges start to set.

9. Sprinkle shredded cheese over the top of the frittata.
10. Transfer the skillet to the preheated oven and bake for 12-15 minutes until the frittata is set in the center and the cheese is melted and bubbly.
11. Remove from the oven, let it cool for a few minutes, then slice and serve.

    Nutritional info: (per serving)

- Calories: 220
- Total Fat: 16g
- Saturated Fat: 5g
- Carbohydrates: 4g
- Fiber: 1g
- Protein: 15g

Peanut Butter Banana Toast

Preparation time: 5 minutes

Number of servings: 2

Ingredients:

- 4 slices of whole-grain bread, toasted
- 2 tablespoons peanut butter
- 1 large ripe banana, thinly sliced
- Honey or cinnamon (optional)

Directions:

1. Spread peanut butter evenly on the toasted bread slices.
2. Place thinly sliced banana on top of the peanut butter layer.

3. Drizzle honey or sprinkle cinnamon over the toast if desired.
4. Serve immediately and enjoy this simple and delicious breakfast!

Nutritional info: (per serving)

- Calories: 290
- Total Fat: 11g
- Saturated Fat: 2g
- Carbohydrates: 42g
- Fiber: 6g
- Protein: 10g

Breakfast Tacos with Beans and Salsa

Preparation time: 10 minutes

Cooking time: 10 minutes

Number of servings: 2

Ingredients:

- 4 small flour or corn tortillas
- 1 cup cooked black beans (canned or homemade)
- 1/2 cup salsa (store-bought or homemade)
- 2 large eggs
- 1/4 cup shredded cheese
- Fresh cilantro or green onions for garnish (optional)
- Salt and pepper to taste
- Cooking oil

Directions:

1. Heat the tortillas in a dry skillet or microwave until warm and pliable.
2. Warm the black beans in a small saucepan over medium heat.
3. In another skillet, heat a bit of oil over medium heat.
4. Crack the eggs into the skillet and fry to your preferred doneness.
5. Season the eggs with salt and pepper.
6. Assemble the tacos: Spread a spoonful of black beans on each tortilla, place a fried egg on top, spoon salsa over the eggs, and sprinkle shredded cheese.
7. Garnish with fresh cilantro or green onions if desired.
8. Serve the breakfast tacos immediately.

Nutritional info: (per serving, 2 tacos)

- Calories: 380
- Total Fat: 14g
- Saturated Fat: 4g
- Carbohydrates: 47g
- Fiber: 11g
- Protein: 19g

Apple Cinnamon Oatmeal

Preparation time: 5 minutes

Cooking time: 10 minutes

Number of servings: 2

Ingredients:

- 1 cup rolled oats
- 2 cups water or milk (almond milk, dairy milk, or any plant-based milk)
- 1 apple, peeled, cored, and chopped
- 1 teaspoon ground cinnamon
- 2 tablespoons maple syrup or honey (optional)
- Chopped nuts or raisins for topping (optional)

Directions:

1. In a saucepan, bring water or milk to a boil.
2. Stir in rolled oats, chopped apple, ground cinnamon, and maple syrup or honey if using.
3. Reduce the heat to medium-low and simmer for about 5-7 minutes, stirring occasionally, until the oats are cooked and the mixture thickens.

4. Once done, remove the oatmeal from heat and let it sit for a minute to thicken further.
5. Serve the apple cinnamon oatmeal in bowls, topping with chopped nuts or raisins if desired.

Nutritional info: (per serving)

- Calories: 250
- Total Fat: 3g
- Saturated Fat: 0.5g
- Carbohydrates: 50g
- Fiber: 7g
- Protein: 6g

Zucchini Fritters

Preparation time: 15 minutes

Cooking time: 15 minutes

Number of servings: 4

Ingredients:

- 2 medium zucchinis, grated
- 1/2 cup breadcrumbs or panko breadcrumbs
- 1/4 cup grated Parmesan cheese (optional)
- 2 cloves garlic, minced
- 1/4 cup chopped fresh parsley
- 2 large eggs, beaten
- Salt and pepper to taste
- Olive oil for frying

Directions:

1. Place the grated zucchini in a colander, sprinkle with salt, and let it sit for 10 minutes to release

excess moisture. Then squeeze out the liquid using a clean kitchen towel or paper towels.

2. In a mixing bowl, combine the grated zucchini, breadcrumbs, Parmesan cheese (if using), minced garlic, chopped parsley, beaten eggs, salt, and pepper.

3. Mix everything until well combined.

4. Heat olive oil in a skillet over medium heat.

5. Spoon the zucchini mixture into the skillet to form fritters, flattening them with a spatula.

6. Cook the fritters for about 3-4 minutes on each side until they are golden brown and crispy.

7. Once cooked, transfer the fritters to a paper towel-lined plate to remove excess oil.

8. Serve the zucchini fritters warm.

Nutritional info: (per serving)

- Calories: 120
- Total Fat: 5g
- Saturated Fat: 1g
- Carbohydrates: 15g
- Fiber: 2g
- Protein: 6g

Vegan Breakfast Sandwich

Preparation time: 10 minutes

Cooking time: 10 minutes

Number of servings: 2

Ingredients:

- 4 slices whole-grain bread or English muffins

- 1 block firm tofu, drained and sliced into 4 rectangles
- 2 tablespoons olive oil
- 1/2 teaspoon turmeric powder
- Salt and pepper to taste
- 2 slices vegan cheese (optional)
- 1 avocado, sliced
- Tomato slices
- Baby spinach or lettuce leaves
- Vegan mayo or your favorite spread

Directions:

1. Heat olive oil in a skillet over medium heat.
2. Sprinkle turmeric powder, salt, and pepper on both sides of the tofu slices.

3. Cook the tofu slices in the skillet for 3-4 minutes on each side until they are golden brown and heated through.
4. Optional: Place a slice of vegan cheese on each tofu slice to melt slightly.
5. Toast the bread slices or English muffins.
6. Assemble the sandwiches: Spread vegan mayo or your preferred spread on the toasted bread.
7. Layer the tofu slices with melted cheese (if using), avocado slices, tomato slices, and baby spinach or lettuce leaves.
8. Top with the remaining slices of bread to complete the sandwiches.
9. Cut the sandwiches in half and serve immediately.

Nutritional info: (per serving)

- Calories: 380
- Total Fat: 22g
- Saturated Fat: 4g
- Carbohydrates: 34g
- Fiber: 9g
- Protein: 15g

Cranberry Orange Scones

Preparation time: 15 minutes

Cooking time: 15 minutes

Number of servings: 8

Ingredients:

- 2 cups all-purpose flour
- 1/3 cup granulated sugar

- 1 tablespoon baking powder

- 1/2 teaspoon salt

- Zest of 1 orange

- 1/2 cup cold unsalted butter, cubed

- 1/2 cup dried cranberries

- 1/2 cup milk or heavy cream

- 1 large egg

- 1 teaspoon vanilla extract

- Additional sugar for sprinkling (optional)

Directions:

1. Preheat the oven to 400°F (200°C) and line a baking sheet with parchment paper.

2. In a large bowl, whisk together the flour, sugar, baking powder, salt, and orange zest.

3. Add the cubed butter to the dry ingredients. Use a pastry cutter or fork to cut the butter into the flour mixture until it resembles coarse crumbs.
4. Stir in the dried cranberries.
5. In a separate bowl, whisk together the milk or cream, egg, and vanilla extract.
6. Pour the wet ingredients into the dry ingredients and mix until just combined. Be careful not to overmix.
7. Transfer the dough to a floured surface and pat it into a circle about 1 inch thick.
8. Cut the dough into 8 wedges and place them on the prepared baking sheet.
9. Optional: Sprinkle the tops of the scones with a little sugar for added sweetness.

10. Bake for 12-15 minutes or until the scones are golden brown.

11. Allow the scones to cool on a wire rack before serving.

    Nutritional info: (per serving)

- Calories: 280

- Total Fat: 12g

- Saturated Fat: 7g

- Carbohydrates: 38g

- Fiber: 1g

- Protein: 4g

Overnight Oats with Fruit

Preparation time: 5 minutes (plus chilling time)

Number of servings: 2

Ingredients:

- 1 cup rolled oats
- 1 cup milk (almond milk, dairy milk, or any plant-based milk)
- 1 tablespoon chia seeds
- 1 tablespoon maple syrup or honey
- 1/2 teaspoon vanilla extract
- Mixed fruits (berries, sliced bananas, diced apples, etc.) for topping
- Nuts, seeds, or granola for topping (optional)

Directions:

1. In a jar or bowl, combine rolled oats, milk, chia seeds, maple syrup or honey, and vanilla extract.

2. Stir well to combine all ingredients thoroughly.
3. Cover the jar or bowl and refrigerate it overnight or for at least 4 hours to allow the oats to soak and soften.
4. In the morning, give the overnight oats a stir.
5. Top the oats with mixed fruits, nuts, seeds, or granola before serving.

Nutritional info: (per serving, without toppings)

- Calories: 250
- Total Fat: 5g
- Saturated Fat: 1g
- Carbohydrates: 45g
- Fiber: 6g
- Protein: 8g

Caprese Breakfast Sandwich

Preparation time: 10 minutes

Cooking time: 5 minutes

Number of servings: 2

Ingredients:

- 4 slices of ciabatta bread or your choice of bread, toasted
- 4 slices of ripe tomato
- 4 slices of fresh mozzarella cheese
- 4 fresh basil leaves
- 2 large eggs
- Olive oil for frying eggs
- Salt and pepper to taste

- Balsamic glaze or balsamic reduction (optional)

Directions:

1. Heat a little olive oil in a skillet over medium heat.
2. Crack the eggs into the skillet and fry them to your desired doneness. Season with salt and pepper.
3. While the eggs are cooking, assemble the sandwiches: On two slices of toasted bread, layer tomato slices, fresh mozzarella slices, and basil leaves.
4. Once the eggs are cooked, place one fried egg on top of each sandwich.
5. Optionally, drizzle balsamic glaze or balsamic reduction over the sandwiches for added flavor.

6. Top each sandwich with the remaining slices of toasted bread.

7. Serve the Caprese breakfast sandwiches immediately.

Nutritional info: (per serving)

- Calories: 400
- Total Fat: 20g
- Saturated Fat: 9g
- Carbohydrates: 30g
- Fiber: 4g
- Protein: 20g

Sweet Potato and Black Bean Hash

Preparation time: 15 minutes

Cooking time: 20 minutes

Number of servings: 4

Ingredients:

- 2 medium sweet potatoes, peeled and diced
- 1 can (15 oz) black beans, drained and rinsed
- 1 red bell pepper, diced
- 1 small onion, diced
- 2 cloves garlic, minced
- 1 teaspoon ground cumin
- 1/2 teaspoon paprika
- Salt and pepper to taste
- 2 tablespoons olive oil
- Fresh cilantro for garnish (optional)

Directions:

1. Heat olive oil in a skillet over medium-high heat.
2. Add diced sweet potatoes to the skillet and cook for about 8-10 minutes until they start to soften and brown.
3. Add diced onion and red bell pepper to the skillet and sauté for an additional 3-4 minutes until the vegetables are tender.
4. Stir in minced garlic, ground cumin, paprika, salt, and pepper. Cook for 1-2 minutes until the spices become fragrant.
5. Add the black beans to the skillet and cook for another 2-3 minutes until everything is heated through.
6. Taste and adjust seasoning if needed.

7. Remove from heat and garnish with fresh cilantro if desired.
8. Serve the sweet potato and black bean hash hot.

Nutritional info: (per serving)

- Calories: 280
- Total Fat: 7g
- Saturated Fat: 1g
- Carbohydrates: 48g
- Fiber: 11g
- Protein: 9g

Broccoli and Cheese Quiche

Preparation time: 15 minutes

Cooking time: 40 minutes

Number of servings: 6

Ingredients:

- 1 pie crust (store-bought or homemade)
- 1 1/2 cups broccoli florets, blanched and chopped
- 1 cup shredded cheddar cheese
- 4 large eggs
- 1 cup milk or heavy cream
- 1/2 teaspoon garlic powder
- Salt and pepper to taste
- Pinch of nutmeg (optional)

Directions:

1. Preheat the oven to 375°F (190°C).

2. Place the pie crust in a pie dish and crimp the edges.

3. Spread chopped broccoli florets and shredded cheddar cheese evenly over the pie crust.

4. In a bowl, whisk together eggs, milk or cream, garlic powder, salt, pepper, and nutmeg if using.

5. Pour the egg mixture over the broccoli and cheese in the pie crust.

6. Place the quiche in the oven and bake for 35-40 minutes or until the center is set and the crust is golden brown.

7. Remove from the oven and let it cool for a few minutes before slicing.

8. Serve warm or at room temperature.

    Nutritional info: (per serving)

- Calories: 300
- Total Fat: 20g
- Saturated Fat: 9g
- Carbohydrates: 18g
- Fiber: 2g
- Protein: 13g

Mango Coconut Chia Pudding

Preparation time: 5 minutes (plus chilling time)

Number of servings: 2

Ingredients:

- 1/4 cup chia seeds
- 1 cup coconut milk
- 1 ripe mango, peeled and diced

- 1 tablespoon honey or maple syrup (optional)
- Shredded coconut or sliced almonds for topping (optional)

Directions:

1. In a bowl or jar, mix together chia seeds and coconut milk.
2. Stir well to combine and ensure no clumps of chia seeds remain.
3. Cover the bowl or jar and refrigerate for at least 2 hours or overnight to allow the mixture to thicken.
4. In a blender, puree half of the diced mango until smooth. Set aside.
5. Once the chia pudding has set, layer it in serving glasses or bowls: Start with a layer of chia pudding, followed by a layer of mango

puree, and continue layering until the glasses are filled.

6. Optionally, drizzle honey or maple syrup over the top and garnish with shredded coconut or sliced almonds.

7. Serve the mango coconut chia pudding chilled. Nutritional info: (per serving, without toppings)

- Calories: 250
- Total Fat: 18g
- Saturated Fat: 10g
- Carbohydrates: 20g
- Fiber: 8g
- Protein: 4g

Ricotta and Berry-Stuffed Crepes

Preparation time: 20 minutes

Cooking time: 20 minutes

Number of servings: 4

Ingredients:

For the Crepes:

- 1 cup all-purpose flour
- 2 large eggs
- 1 cup milk
- 1/4 cup water
- 2 tablespoons melted butter
- Pinch of salt
- 1 tablespoon granulated sugar (optional)
- Butter or oil for cooking

For the Filling:

- 1 cup ricotta cheese
- 1 tablespoon honey or maple syrup (optional)
- 1 teaspoon vanilla extract
- 2 cups mixed berries (strawberries, blueberries, raspberries)
- Powdered sugar for dusting (optional)
- Whipped cream for topping (optional)

Directions:

Prepare the Crepe Batter:

1. In a blender or mixing bowl, combine flour, eggs, milk, water, melted butter, salt, and granulated sugar (if using). Blend or whisk until smooth.
2. Let the batter rest for at least 15 minutes.

Cook the Crepes:

1. Heat a non-stick skillet or crepe pan over medium heat.
2. Add a small amount of butter or oil to coat the pan.
3. Pour a ladleful of crepe batter into the hot pan and swirl it around to coat the bottom evenly.
4. Cook the crepe for about 1-2 minutes until the edges start to lift and the bottom is lightly golden.
5. Flip the crepe and cook for an additional 1 minute on the other side.
6. Repeat with the remaining batter, stacking the cooked crepes on a plate as you go. You should get around 8 crepes.

Prepare the Filling:

1. In a bowl, mix the ricotta cheese with honey or maple syrup (if using) and vanilla extract until well combined.
2. Spread a generous spoonful of the ricotta mixture onto each crepe.
3. Add a handful of mixed berries on top of the ricotta filling.

Roll the Crepes:

1. Fold the sides of each crepe over the filling, then roll them up to enclose the ricotta and berries.
2. Serve:
3. Place the stuffed crepes on serving plates.
4. Dust with powdered sugar if desired and top with whipped cream.

5. Optionally, add a few extra berries on top for garnish.

   Nutritional info: (per serving)

- Calories: 320
- Total Fat: 15g
- Saturated Fat: 8g
- Carbohydrates: 35g
- Fiber: 4g
- Protein: 11g

Chapter 5

Wholesome Lunches

Veggie Wrap with Hummus

Preparation time: 15 minutes

Cooking time: N/A

Number of servings: 2

Ingredients:

- 2 large tortillas or wraps
- 1 cup hummus
- 1 cup mixed salad greens
- 1 cucumber, thinly sliced

- 1 large carrot, grated
- 1 bell pepper, thinly sliced
- 1/2 red onion, thinly sliced
- Optional: feta cheese or tofu (crumbled or sliced)

Directions:

1. Lay out the tortillas on a flat surface.
2. Spread a generous layer of hummus evenly over each tortilla.
3. Layer the mixed salad greens, cucumber slices, grated carrot, bell pepper slices, red onion, and any optional ingredients (feta cheese or tofu) over the hummus.
4. Fold in the sides of the tortilla and roll it up tightly, securing it with a toothpick if needed.

5. Slice the wraps in half diagonally and serve.

   Nutritional info: (per serving)

- Calories: 320
- Total Fat: 12g
- Saturated Fat: 2g
- Cholesterol: 0mg
- Sodium: 670mg
- Total Carbohydrate: 45g
- Dietary Fiber: 10g
- Total Sugars: 5g
- Protein: 12g

Caprese Salad

Preparation time: 10 minutes

Cooking time: N/A

Number of servings: 4

Ingredients:

- 4 ripe tomatoes, sliced
- 1 pound fresh mozzarella cheese, sliced
- 1/2 cup fresh basil leaves
- 2 tablespoons balsamic glaze
- Salt and pepper to taste

Directions:

1. Arrange the tomato and mozzarella slices alternately on a serving platter.
2. Tuck basil leaves between the tomato and mozzarella slices.
3. Drizzle the balsamic glaze over the salad.

4. Season with salt and pepper to taste.
5. Serve immediately.

   Nutritional info: (per serving)

- Calories: 320
- Total Fat: 20g
- Saturated Fat: 12g
- Cholesterol: 60mg
- Sodium: 560mg
- Total Carbohydrate: 8g
- Dietary Fiber: 2g
- Total Sugars: 5g
- Protein: 28g

Lentil Soup

Preparation time: 15 minutes

Cooking time: 45 minutes

Number of servings: 6

Ingredients:

- 1 cup dried lentils, rinsed and drained
- 1 onion, finely chopped
- 2 carrots, diced
- 2 celery stalks, diced
- 3 cloves garlic, minced
- 6 cups vegetable broth
- 1 can (14 oz) diced tomatoes
- 1 teaspoon ground cumin
- 1 teaspoon smoked paprika
- Salt and pepper to taste

- Fresh parsley for garnish

  Directions:

1. In a large pot, sauté the onion, carrots, celery, and garlic until softened.
2. Add the lentils, vegetable broth, diced tomatoes, cumin, smoked paprika, salt, and pepper to the pot.
3. Bring the mixture to a boil, then reduce heat and let it simmer for about 40-45 minutes until the lentils are tender.
4. Adjust seasoning if needed.
5. Serve hot, garnished with fresh parsley.

   Nutritional info: (per serving)

- Calories: 220
- Total Fat: 1.5g

- Saturated Fat: 0g

- Cholesterol: 0mg

- Sodium: 780mg

- Total Carbohydrate: 40g

- Dietary Fiber: 16g

- Total Sugars: 7g

- Protein: 14g

Veggie Sushi Rolls

Preparation time: 30 minutes

Cooking time: 20 minutes

Number of servings: 4-6 rolls

Ingredients:

- 2 cups sushi rice

- 4 cups water

- 1/3 cup rice vinegar

- 2 tablespoons sugar

- 1 teaspoon salt

- Nori seaweed sheets

- Assorted veggies (cucumber, avocado, bell peppers, carrots, etc.)

- Soy sauce, pickled ginger, wasabi (for serving)

Directions:

1. Rinse the sushi rice until the water runs clear. Cook the rice with 4 cups of water in a rice cooker or on the stovetop according to package instructions.

2. In a small saucepan, heat the rice vinegar, sugar, and salt until dissolved. Let it cool.

3. Spread the cooked rice onto a baking sheet and gently fold in the vinegar mixture to season the rice. Let it cool to room temperature.
4. Place a nori sheet on a bamboo sushi mat. Wet your hands and spread a thin layer of rice on the nori, leaving a 1-inch border at the top.
5. Arrange your choice of veggies in a line across the rice.
6. Roll the nori tightly using the sushi mat, sealing the edge with a bit of water.
7. Repeat with the remaining ingredients.
8. Slice the rolls into bite-sized pieces using a sharp knife.
9. Serve with soy sauce, pickled ginger, and wasabi.

Nutritional info: (per serving, assuming 1 roll)

- Calories: 200

- Total Fat: 1g

- Saturated Fat: 0g

- Cholesterol: 0mg

- Sodium: 400mg

- Total Carbohydrate: 44g

- Dietary Fiber: 2g

- Total Sugars: 2g

- Protein: 4g

Greek Salad with Feta

Preparation time: 15 minutes

Cooking time: N/A

Number of servings: 4

Ingredients:

- 4 cups mixed salad greens
- 1 cucumber, diced
- 1 cup cherry tomatoes, halved
- 1/2 red onion, thinly sliced
- 1/2 cup Kalamata olives
- 1/2 cup crumbled feta cheese
- 1/4 cup extra virgin olive oil
- 2 tablespoons red wine vinegar
- 1 teaspoon dried oregano
- Salt and pepper to taste

Directions:

1. In a large bowl, combine the mixed salad greens, diced cucumber, cherry tomatoes, red onion, and Kalamata olives.

2. In a small bowl, whisk together the olive oil, red wine vinegar, dried oregano, salt, and pepper to make the dressing.
3. Drizzle the dressing over the salad and toss gently to coat.
4. Sprinkle the crumbled feta cheese over the top before serving.

    Nutritional info: (per serving)

- Calories: 250
- Total Fat: 20g
- Saturated Fat: 5g
- Cholesterol: 20mg
- Sodium: 480mg
- Total Carbohydrate: 12g
- Dietary Fiber: 3g

- Total Sugars: 6g
- Protein: 6g

Chickpea Salad Sandwich

Preparation time: 15 minutes

Cooking time: N/A

Number of servings: 4

Ingredients:

- 2 cans (15 oz each) chickpeas, drained and rinsed
- 1/4 cup mayonnaise or vegan mayo
- 2 tablespoons Dijon mustard
- 1 stalk celery, finely chopped
- 1/4 cup red onion, finely chopped

- 1/4 cup fresh parsley, chopped
- Salt and pepper to taste
- Bread or sandwich rolls
- Lettuce, tomato slices (optional for sandwich filling)

Directions:

1. In a mixing bowl, lightly mash the chickpeas with a fork or potato masher, leaving some chunks for texture.
2. Add mayonnaise, Dijon mustard, chopped celery, red onion, parsley, salt, and pepper to the chickpeas. Mix until well combined.
3. Toast the bread or sandwich rolls if desired.
4. Spread the chickpea salad onto the bread or rolls. Add lettuce and tomato slices if using.

5. Assemble the sandwiches and serve.

   Nutritional info: (per serving, without bread or additional fillings)

- Calories: 230
- Total Fat: 10g
- Saturated Fat: 1g
- Cholesterol: 5mg
- Sodium: 420mg
- Total Carbohydrate: 27g
- Dietary Fiber: 8g
- Total Sugars: 3g
- Protein: 9g

Ratatouille

Preparation time: 20 minutes

Cooking time: 40 minutes

Number of servings: 4

Ingredients:

- 1 eggplant, diced
- 2 zucchinis, sliced
- 1 bell pepper, diced
- 1 onion, chopped
- 2 cloves garlic, minced
- 3 tomatoes, diced
- 2 tablespoons tomato paste
- 2 tablespoons olive oil
- 1 teaspoon dried thyme
- 1 teaspoon dried basil

- Salt and pepper to taste
- Fresh basil for garnish (optional)

Directions:

1. Heat olive oil in a large pan over medium heat. Add the onion and garlic, sauté until softened.
2. Add the diced eggplant, zucchini, and bell pepper to the pan. Cook until slightly tender.
3. Stir in the diced tomatoes, tomato paste, dried thyme, dried basil, salt, and pepper. Mix well.
4. Cover the pan and simmer for 20-25 minutes, stirring occasionally, until the vegetables are cooked through but not mushy.
5. Adjust seasoning if needed.
6. Garnish with fresh basil if desired before serving.

Nutritional info: (per serving)

- Calories: 120
- Total Fat: 6g
- Saturated Fat: 1g
- Cholesterol: 0mg
- Sodium: 260mg
- Total Carbohydrate: 16g
- Dietary Fiber: 6g
- Total Sugars: 9g
- Protein: 3g

Quinoa-Stuffed Bell Peppers

Preparation time: 20 minutes

Cooking time: 40 minutes

Number of servings: 4

Ingredients:

- 4 large bell peppers, tops removed and seeds discarded
- 1 cup quinoa, rinsed
- 2 cups vegetable broth or water
- 1 can (15 oz) black beans, drained and rinsed
- 1 cup corn kernels (fresh or frozen)
- 1 cup diced tomatoes
- 1 teaspoon cumin
- 1 teaspoon chili powder
- Salt and pepper to taste
- 1/2 cup shredded cheese (optional)

Directions:

1. Preheat the oven to 375°F (190°C).
2. In a pot, bring the vegetable broth or water to a boil. Add quinoa, reduce heat, cover, and simmer for 15-20 minutes until the liquid is absorbed and quinoa is cooked.
3. In a mixing bowl, combine the cooked quinoa, black beans, corn kernels, diced tomatoes, cumin, chili powder, salt, and pepper.
4. Stuff each bell pepper with the quinoa mixture and place them in a baking dish.
5. Optionally, sprinkle shredded cheese on top of each stuffed pepper.
6. Bake in the preheated oven for 20-25 minutes until the peppers are tender and the filling is heated through.
7. Serve hot.

Nutritional info: (per serving)

- Calories: 320
- Total Fat: 5g
- Saturated Fat: 1.5g
- Cholesterol: 5mg
- Sodium: 520mg
- Total Carbohydrate: 58g
- Dietary Fiber: 12g
- Total Sugars: 10g
- Protein: 14g

Spinach and Cheese Quesadilla

Preparation time: 10 minutes

Cooking time: 10 minutes

Number of servings: 2

Ingredients:

- 4 large flour tortillas
- 2 cups baby spinach leaves
- 1 cup shredded cheese (cheddar, Monterey Jack, or a blend)
- Olive oil or butter for cooking
- Salsa, sour cream, guacamole (for serving, optional)

Directions:

1. Heat a skillet or griddle over medium heat.
2. Place one tortilla on the skillet. Sprinkle half of the shredded cheese evenly over the tortilla.
3. Layer half of the baby spinach leaves on top of the cheese.

4. Place another tortilla on top to cover the filling.
5. Cook for 2-3 minutes on each side until the tortilla turns golden brown and the cheese melts.
6. Repeat the process for the second quesadilla.
7. Cut each quesadilla into wedges and serve hot with salsa, sour cream, or guacamole if desired.

Nutritional info: (per serving)

- Calories: 450
- Total Fat: 20g
- Saturated Fat: 10g
- Cholesterol: 45mg
- Sodium: 680mg
- Total Carbohydrate: 48g
- Dietary Fiber: 4g

- Total Sugars: 2g
- Protein: 18g

Vegetarian Chili

Preparation time: 15 minutes

Cooking time: 45 minutes

Number of servings: 6

Ingredients:

- 2 tablespoons olive oil
- 1 onion, chopped
- 3 cloves garlic, minced
- 1 bell pepper, diced
- 2 carrots, diced
- 2 celery stalks, diced

- 1 can (15 oz) black beans, drained and rinsed
- 1 can (15 oz) kidney beans, drained and rinsed
- 1 can (15 oz) diced tomatoes
- 2 cups vegetable broth
- 2 tablespoons chili powder
- 1 teaspoon ground cumin
- 1 teaspoon paprika
- Salt and pepper to taste
- Optional toppings: shredded cheese, sour cream, chopped cilantro, sliced jalapeños

Directions:

1. Heat olive oil in a large pot over medium heat. Add onion and garlic, sauté until softened.
2. Add bell pepper, carrots, and celery. Cook for 5-7 minutes until vegetables begin to soften.

3. Stir in black beans, kidney beans, diced tomatoes, vegetable broth, chili powder, cumin, paprika, salt, and pepper.
4. Bring the chili to a simmer, then reduce heat and let it cook for 30-40 minutes, stirring occasionally, until the flavors meld and the vegetables are tender.
5. Adjust seasoning if needed.
6. Serve hot with optional toppings.

Nutritional info: (per serving)

- Calories: 240
- Total Fat: 6g
- Saturated Fat: 1g
- Cholesterol: 0mg
- Sodium: 680mg

- Total Carbohydrate: 38g
- Dietary Fiber: 12g
- Total Sugars: 6g
- Protein: 11g

Tomato Basil Mozzarella Skewers

Preparation time: 15 minutes

Cooking time: N/A

Number of servings: 4

Ingredients:

- 2 cups cherry tomatoes
- 8 ounces fresh mozzarella balls
- Fresh basil leaves
- Balsamic glaze

- Olive oil (optional)
- Salt and pepper to taste

Directions:

1. On wooden skewers or toothpicks, thread a cherry tomato, a folded basil leaf, and a mozzarella ball.
2. Repeat until the skewer is filled, leaving some space at each end.
3. Arrange the skewers on a serving platter.
4. Drizzle with balsamic glaze and olive oil if desired.
5. Season with salt and pepper to taste.
6. Serve immediately.

Nutritional info: (per serving)

- Calories: 180

- Total Fat: 12g

- Saturated Fat: 6g

- Cholesterol: 30mg

- Sodium: 300mg

- Total Carbohydrate: 6g

- Dietary Fiber: 1g

- Total Sugars: 3g

- Protein: 10g

Falafel with Tzatziki Sauce

Preparation time: 20 minutes

Cooking time: 15 minutes

Number of servings: Makes about 20 falafel

Ingredients:

For Falafel:

- 2 cans (15 oz each) chickpeas, drained and rinsed
- 1 small onion, chopped
- 3 cloves garlic, minced
- 1/4 cup fresh parsley, chopped
- 2 tablespoons fresh cilantro, chopped
- 2 teaspoons ground cumin
- 2 teaspoons ground coriander
- 1 teaspoon baking powder
- 4 tablespoons all-purpose flour or chickpea flour
- Salt and pepper to taste
- Oil for frying

For Tzatziki Sauce:

- 1 cup Greek yogurt
- 1 cucumber, grated and drained
- 2 cloves garlic, minced
- 1 tablespoon lemon juice
- 1 tablespoon olive oil
- 1 tablespoon fresh dill, chopped
- Salt and pepper to taste

Directions:

1. In a food processor, combine chickpeas, onion, garlic, parsley, cilantro, cumin, coriander, baking powder, flour, salt, and pepper. Pulse until mixture becomes a coarse paste.
2. Shape the mixture into small balls or patties.

3. Heat oil in a frying pan over medium-high heat. Fry the falafel in batches until golden brown and crispy, about 3-4 minutes per side. Drain on paper towels.

4. For the tzatziki sauce, mix together Greek yogurt, grated cucumber, garlic, lemon juice, olive oil, dill, salt, and pepper in a bowl. Refrigerate until ready to serve.

5. Serve the falafel hot with tzatziki sauce on the side.

    Nutritional info: (per serving, assuming 5 falafel and 2 tablespoons of tzatziki sauce)

- Calories: 320
- Total Fat: 15g
- Saturated Fat: 3g

- Cholesterol: 5mg
- Sodium: 480mg
- Total Carbohydrate: 35g
- Dietary Fiber: 9g
- Total Sugars: 6g
- Protein: 15g

Broccoli Cheddar Soup

Preparation time: 15 minutes

Cooking time: 25 minutes

Number of servings: 4

Ingredients:

- 2 tablespoons butter
- 1 onion, diced

- 2 cloves garlic, minced

- 3 cups broccoli florets

- 2 cups vegetable or chicken broth

- 1 cup milk or cream

- 1 cup shredded cheddar cheese

- Salt and pepper to taste

- Optional: Red pepper flakes or nutmeg for seasoning

Directions:

1. In a pot, melt butter over medium heat. Add diced onion and garlic, sauté until softened.

2. Add broccoli florets and broth to the pot. Bring to a simmer and cook for 10-15 minutes until the broccoli is tender.

3. Use an immersion blender or transfer the mixture to a blender to puree until smooth.
4. Return the pureed mixture to the pot. Stir in milk or cream and shredded cheddar cheese, heating gently until the cheese melts.
5. Season with salt, pepper, and any additional seasoning if desired.
6. Serve hot.

Nutritional info: (per serving)

- Calories: 260
- Total Fat: 18g
- Saturated Fat: 11g
- Cholesterol: 55mg
- Sodium: 520mg
- Total Carbohydrate: 15g

- Dietary Fiber: 3g
- Total Sugars: 6g
- Protein: 10g

Spinach and Mushroom Lasagna

Preparation time: 30 minutes

Cooking time: 1 hour

Number of servings: 8

Ingredients:

- 12 lasagna noodles, cooked according to package instructions
- 1 tablespoon olive oil
- 1 onion, chopped
- 3 cloves garlic, minced

- 8 oz mushrooms, sliced

- 6 cups fresh spinach leaves

- 2 cups ricotta cheese

- 1/2 cup grated Parmesan cheese

- 3 cups marinara sauce

- 2 cups shredded mozzarella cheese

- Salt and pepper to taste

- Fresh basil for garnish (optional)

Directions:

1. Preheat oven to 375°F (190°C).
2. Heat olive oil in a pan over medium heat. Add onion and garlic, sauté until softened.
3. Add sliced mushrooms and cook until they release their moisture, then add fresh spinach.

Cook until spinach wilts. Season with salt and pepper.

4. In a bowl, mix together ricotta cheese and grated Parmesan cheese.
5. Spread a thin layer of marinara sauce in the bottom of a baking dish.
6. Layer cooked lasagna noodles, followed by ricotta mixture, mushroom-spinach mixture, marinara sauce, and shredded mozzarella cheese. Repeat layers, ending with mozzarella cheese on top.
7. Cover with foil and bake for 30 minutes. Remove foil and bake for an additional 15-20 minutes until cheese is bubbly and golden.

8. Let it rest for 10 minutes before slicing. Garnish with fresh basil if desired before serving.

Nutritional info: (per serving)

- Calories: 380
- Total Fat: 16g
- Saturated Fat: 8g
- Cholesterol: 45mg
- Sodium: 750mg
- Total Carbohydrate: 38g
- Dietary Fiber: 4g
- Total Sugars: 7g
- Protein: 20g

Cauliflower Tacos

Preparation time: 20 minutes

Cooking time: 20 minutes

Number of servings: 4

Ingredients:

For Cauliflower:

- 1 head cauliflower, cut into florets
- 2 tablespoons olive oil
- 1 tablespoon chili powder
- 1 teaspoon ground cumin
- 1/2 teaspoon smoked paprika
- Salt and pepper to taste

For Tacos:

- 8 small tortillas (corn or flour)
- 1 cup shredded lettuce

- 1 cup diced tomatoes
- 1/2 cup diced red onion
- 1/2 cup chopped cilantro
- Lime wedges for serving
- Optional toppings: salsa, sour cream, avocado slices

Directions:

1. Preheat oven to 425°F (220°C).
2. In a bowl, toss cauliflower florets with olive oil, chili powder, cumin, smoked paprika, salt, and pepper until coated.
3. Spread cauliflower on a baking sheet and roast for 20-25 minutes until tender and slightly crispy.
4. Warm the tortillas in a skillet or microwave.

5. Assemble tacos by filling each tortilla with roasted cauliflower, shredded lettuce, diced tomatoes, red onion, and chopped cilantro.
6. Serve with lime wedges and optional toppings on the side.

   Nutritional info: (per serving, 2 tacos)

- Calories: 280
- Total Fat: 9g
- Saturated Fat: 1g
- Cholesterol: 0mg
- Sodium: 550mg
- Total Carbohydrate: 45g
- Dietary Fiber: 9g
- Total Sugars: 6g
- Protein: 8g

Eggplant Parmesan

Preparation time: 30 minutes

Cooking time: 45 minutes

Number of servings: 4

Ingredients:

- 2 medium eggplants, sliced into 1/2-inch rounds
- Salt
- 2 cups breadcrumbs
- 1 cup grated Parmesan cheese
- 2 eggs, beaten
- 2 cups marinara sauce
- 2 cups shredded mozzarella cheese

- Fresh basil leaves for garnish

Directions:

1. Preheat the oven to 375°F (190°C).
2. Place eggplant slices on a baking sheet and sprinkle with salt. Let them sit for 15-20 minutes to release moisture, then pat dry with paper towels.
3. In one bowl, mix breadcrumbs and grated Parmesan cheese. In another bowl, beat the eggs.
4. Dip each eggplant slice into the beaten eggs, then coat it with the breadcrumb mixture.
5. Place the coated eggplant slices on a baking sheet lined with parchment paper. Bake for 20-25 minutes until golden and crisp.

6. In a baking dish, spread a thin layer of marinara sauce. Arrange half of the baked eggplant slices over the sauce.

7. Top the eggplant with more marinara sauce and shredded mozzarella cheese. Repeat with another layer of eggplant, sauce, and cheese.

8. Bake for an additional 20 minutes until the cheese is melted and bubbly.

9. Garnish with fresh basil leaves before serving.

Nutritional info: (per serving)

- Calories: 380
- Total Fat: 18g
- Saturated Fat: 9g
- Cholesterol: 110mg
- Sodium: 1050mg

- Total Carbohydrate: 32g
- Dietary Fiber: 8g
- Total Sugars: 10g
- Protein: 23g

Veggie Burger with Avocado

Preparation time: 20 minutes

Cooking time: 10 minutes

Number of servings: 4

Ingredients:

- 4 veggie burger patties (store-bought or homemade)
- 4 hamburger buns
- 1 avocado, sliced

- Lettuce leaves
- Tomato slices
- Red onion slices
- Optional toppings: cheese slices, ketchup, mustard, mayo

Directions:

1. Cook the veggie burger patties according to package instructions or recipe.
2. Toast the hamburger buns if desired.
3. Assemble the burgers by placing a veggie patty on the bottom half of each bun.
4. Top with avocado slices, lettuce, tomato, red onion, and any additional toppings of your choice.
5. Cover with the top half of the bun.

6. Serve the veggie burgers immediately.

   Nutritional info: (per serving)

- Calories: 320
- Total Fat: 14g
- Saturated Fat: 2g
- Cholesterol: 0mg
- Sodium: 680mg
- Total Carbohydrate: 42g
- Dietary Fiber: 8g
- Total Sugars: 6g
- Protein: 10g

Mushroom Risotto

Preparation time: 10 minutes

Cooking time: 30 minutes

Number of servings: 4

Ingredients:

- 1 1/2 cups Arborio rice
- 4 cups vegetable or chicken broth, kept warm
- 2 tablespoons olive oil
- 1 onion, finely chopped
- 2 cloves garlic, minced
- 8 oz mushrooms (cremini, shiitake, or a mix), sliced
- 1/2 cup dry white wine
- 1/2 cup grated Parmesan cheese
- 2 tablespoons butter
- Salt and pepper to taste

- Fresh parsley for garnish (optional)

Directions:

1. In a large skillet or saucepan, heat olive oil over medium heat. Add chopped onion and garlic, sauté until softened.
2. Add sliced mushrooms and cook until they release their moisture and become golden brown.
3. Stir in Arborio rice and cook for 2-3 minutes until lightly toasted.
4. Pour in the white wine and stir until it evaporates.
5. Begin adding warm broth to the rice mixture, one ladleful at a time, stirring continuously and allowing the liquid to absorb before adding more.

6. Continue this process until the rice is creamy and cooked al dente, about 20-25 minutes.
7. Stir in grated Parmesan cheese and butter. Season with salt and pepper to taste.
8. Garnish with fresh parsley before serving.

Nutritional info: (per serving)

- Calories: 380
- Total Fat: 12g
- Saturated Fat: 5g
- Cholesterol: 20mg
- Sodium: 800mg
- Total Carbohydrate: 55g
- Dietary Fiber: 3g
- Total Sugars: 3g
- Protein: 10g

Pasta Primavera

Preparation time: 15 minutes

Cooking time: 20 minutes

Number of servings: 4

Ingredients:

- 8 oz pasta (linguine or spaghetti)
- 2 tablespoons olive oil
- 3 cloves garlic, minced
- 1 onion, thinly sliced
- 2 carrots, julienned or thinly sliced
- 1 red bell pepper, thinly sliced
- 1 yellow bell pepper, thinly sliced
- 1 cup broccoli florets

- 1 cup cherry tomatoes, halved

- 1/2 cup peas (fresh or frozen)

- 1/4 cup chopped fresh basil or parsley

- Salt and pepper to taste

- Grated Parmesan cheese for serving (optional)

Directions:

1. Cook pasta according to package instructions. Drain and set aside.

2. Heat olive oil in a large skillet over medium heat. Add minced garlic and sauté until fragrant.

3. Add sliced onion and cook until softened, then add carrots, bell peppers, and broccoli. Sauté for 5-7 minutes until vegetables are tender-crisp.

4. Stir in cherry tomatoes and peas. Cook for an additional 2-3 minutes until tomatoes soften.
5. Add cooked pasta to the skillet with the vegetables. Toss everything together.
6. Season with salt, pepper, and chopped basil or parsley.
7. Serve hot, optionally topped with grated Parmesan cheese.

Nutritional info: (per serving)

- Calories: 320
- Total Fat: 8g
- Saturated Fat: 1g
- Cholesterol: 0mg
- Sodium: 40mg
- Total Carbohydrate: 55g

- Dietary Fiber: 7g
- Total Sugars: 8g
- Protein: 9g

Black Bean and Corn Salad

Preparation time: 15 minutes

Cooking time: 0 minutes

Number of servings: 6

Ingredients:

- 2 cans (15 oz each) black beans, drained and rinsed
- 2 cups corn kernels (fresh, canned, or thawed if frozen)
- 1 red bell pepper, diced

- 1/2 red onion, finely chopped
- 1/4 cup chopped fresh cilantro
- 1 jalapeño pepper, seeded and minced (optional)
- Juice of 2 limes
- 2 tablespoons olive oil
- 1 teaspoon ground cumin
- Salt and pepper to taste
- Avocado slices for garnish (optional)

Directions:

1. In a large bowl, combine black beans, corn, diced red bell pepper, chopped red onion, cilantro, and minced jalapeño if using.
2. In a small bowl, whisk together lime juice, olive oil, ground cumin, salt, and pepper.

3. Pour the dressing over the salad ingredients and toss to combine.
4. Garnish with avocado slices if desired.
5. Serve chilled or at room temperature.

   Nutritional info: (per serving)

- Calories: 250
- Total Fat: 6g
- Saturated Fat: 1g
- Cholesterol: 0mg
- Sodium: 390mg
- Total Carbohydrate: 40g
- Dietary Fiber: 12g
- Total Sugars: 4g
- Protein: 11g

Stuffed Portobello Mushrooms

Preparation time: 15 minutes

Cooking time: 20 minutes

Number of servings: 4

Ingredients:

- 4 large portobello mushrooms, stems removed
- 2 tablespoons olive oil
- 2 cloves garlic, minced
- 1/2 onion, diced
- 1 bell pepper, diced
- 1 cup spinach, chopped
- 1/2 cup breadcrumbs
- 1/4 cup grated Parmesan cheese
- Salt and pepper to taste

- Fresh parsley for garnish

Directions:

1. Preheat oven to 375°F (190°C). Place the portobello mushrooms on a baking sheet.
2. Heat olive oil in a skillet over medium heat. Add minced garlic and diced onion, sauté until softened.
3. Add diced bell pepper and chopped spinach. Cook until the vegetables are tender and spinach wilts.
4. Stir in breadcrumbs, grated Parmesan cheese, salt, and pepper. Mix well.
5. Spoon the vegetable mixture evenly into the portobello mushroom caps.
6. Bake for 15-20 minutes until the mushrooms are tender and the stuffing is golden.

7. Garnish with fresh parsley before serving.

   Nutritional info: (per serving)

- Calories: 130
- Total Fat: 6g
- Saturated Fat: 1.5g
- Cholesterol: 5mg
- Sodium: 230mg
- Total Carbohydrate: 15g
- Dietary Fiber: 4g
- Total Sugars: 3g
- Protein: 7g

Sweet Potato and Black Bean Quesadilla

Preparation time: 25 minutes

Cooking time: 20 minutes

Number of servings: 4

Ingredients:

- 2 large sweet potatoes, peeled and diced
- 1 can (15 oz) black beans, drained and rinsed
- 1 teaspoon ground cumin
- 1 teaspoon chili powder
- 1/2 teaspoon smoked paprika
- Salt and pepper to taste
- 8 whole wheat or corn tortillas
- 2 cups shredded cheese (cheddar, Monterey Jack, or a blend)
- Olive oil for cooking

- Optional toppings: salsa, guacamole, sour cream

Directions:

1. Boil or steam the diced sweet potatoes until tender, about 10-15 minutes. Mash them lightly with a fork and set aside.
2. In a bowl, mix the black beans with cumin, chili powder, smoked paprika, salt, and pepper.
3. Lay out half of the tortillas and spread a layer of mashed sweet potatoes onto each one.
4. Top the sweet potatoes with the seasoned black beans and shredded cheese.
5. Place the remaining tortillas on top to create quesadillas.
6. Heat a skillet or griddle over medium heat and lightly brush with olive oil.

7. Cook each quesadilla for 2-3 minutes on each side until the tortillas are golden and the cheese is melted.
8. Cut each quesadilla into wedges and serve with optional toppings.

Nutritional info: (per serving)

- Calories: 450
- Total Fat: 15g
- Saturated Fat: 7g
- Cholesterol: 30mg
- Sodium: 600mg
- Total Carbohydrate: 60g
- Dietary Fiber: 12g
- Total Sugars: 6g
- Protein: 18g

Greek-Style Stuffed Tomatoes

Preparation time: 20 minutes

Cooking time: 40 minutes

Number of servings: 4

Ingredients:

- 4 large tomatoes
- 1 cup cooked rice
- 1/2 cup crumbled feta cheese
- 1/4 cup chopped fresh parsley
- 1/4 cup chopped fresh mint
- 1/4 cup chopped red onion
- 2 tablespoons olive oil
- Salt and pepper to taste

- Lemon wedges for serving

Directions:

1. Preheat the oven to 375°F (190°C).
2. Slice the tops off the tomatoes and scoop out the flesh and seeds, leaving a shell. Reserve the tomato pulp for later use.
3. In a bowl, mix together cooked rice, crumbled feta cheese, chopped parsley, chopped mint, chopped red onion, and a tablespoon of olive oil. Season with salt and pepper.
4. Stuff each hollowed-out tomato with the rice mixture.
5. Place the stuffed tomatoes in a baking dish. Drizzle the remaining olive oil over the top.
6. Bake for 35-40 minutes until the tomatoes are tender and the filling is heated through.

7. Serve hot with lemon wedges on the side.

   Nutritional info: (per serving)

- Calories: 180
- Total Fat: 9g
- Saturated Fat: 3g
- Cholesterol: 15mg
- Sodium: 220mg
- Total Carbohydrate: 20g
- Dietary Fiber: 3g
- Total Sugars: 5g
- Protein: 5g

Spinach and Ricotta Stuffed Shells

Preparation time: 30 minutes

Cooking time: 30 minutes

Number of servings: 6

Ingredients:

- 18 jumbo pasta shells, cooked according to package instructions
- 2 cups ricotta cheese
- 1 cup chopped spinach, cooked and drained
- 1/2 cup grated Parmesan cheese
- 1 egg
- 2 cups marinara sauce
- 1 cup shredded mozzarella cheese
- Salt and pepper to taste
- Fresh basil for garnish

Directions:

1. Preheat the oven to 375°F (190°C).
2. In a bowl, combine ricotta cheese, chopped spinach, grated Parmesan cheese, and beaten egg. Season with salt and pepper.
3. Stuff each cooked pasta shell with the spinach and ricotta mixture.
4. Spread a thin layer of marinara sauce in a baking dish.
5. Arrange the stuffed shells in the dish and top with the remaining marinara sauce.
6. Sprinkle shredded mozzarella cheese over the top.
7. Cover the dish with foil and bake for 20 minutes. Remove the foil and bake for an additional 10 minutes until the cheese is melted and bubbly.

8. Garnish with fresh basil before serving.

   Nutritional info: (per serving, 3 shells)

- Calories: 350
- Total Fat: 14g
- Saturated Fat: 8g
- Cholesterol: 75mg
- Sodium: 560mg
- Total Carbohydrate: 33g
- Dietary Fiber: 3g
- Total Sugars: 6g
- Protein: 20g

Grilled Vegetable Panini

Preparation time: 15 minutes

Cooking time: 10 minutes

Number of servings: 2

Ingredients:

- 1 small zucchini, thinly sliced lengthwise
- 1 small yellow squash, thinly sliced lengthwise
- 1 red bell pepper, sliced into strips
- 1 yellow bell pepper, sliced into strips
- 1 small eggplant, thinly sliced rounds
- 4 slices of bread (ciabatta, sourdough, or your choice)
- 1/2 cup basil pesto
- 4 slices provolone cheese (or cheese of choice)
- Olive oil for brushing
- Salt and pepper to taste

Directions:

1. Preheat a grill pan or an outdoor grill over medium-high heat.
2. Brush the sliced zucchini, yellow squash, bell peppers, and eggplant with olive oil. Season with salt and pepper.
3. Grill the vegetables for 3-4 minutes on each side until they have grill marks and are tender.
4. Spread basil pesto on one side of each slice of bread.
5. On the pesto-spread side of two slices of bread, layer grilled vegetables and provolone cheese. Top with the other two slices of bread, pesto side down.
6. Heat a panini press or a skillet over medium heat.

7. Place the assembled sandwiches onto the press or skillet. If using a skillet, press the sandwiches down with a spatula and cook for 3-4 minutes on each side until the bread is golden and the cheese melts.

8. Once done, remove from heat, slice the sandwiches in half, and serve hot.

   Nutritional info: (per serving)

- Calories: 420
- Total Fat: 22g
- Saturated Fat: 8g
- Cholesterol: 25mg
- Sodium: 780mg
- Total Carbohydrate: 39g
- Dietary Fiber: 6g

- Total Sugars: 9g
- Protein: 19g

Chapter 6

Nourishing Dinners

Vegetable Stir-Fry with Tofu

Preparation time: 15 minutes

Cooking time: 15 minutes

Number of servings: 4

Ingredients:

- 1 block (14 oz) firm tofu, drained and pressed
- 2 tablespoons soy sauce
- 2 tablespoons sesame oil
- 1 tablespoon cornstarch

- 2 tablespoons vegetable oil
- 2 cloves garlic, minced
- 1 tablespoon ginger, grated
- 1 red bell pepper, sliced
- 1 yellow bell pepper, sliced
- 1 cup broccoli florets
- 1 cup snap peas
- 1 carrot, julienned
- 1 cup mushrooms, sliced
- 3 tablespoons hoisin sauce
- Salt and pepper to taste
- Cooked rice for serving

Directions:

1. Preheat your skillet or wok over medium-high heat.

2. Cut the tofu into cubes and toss them in a mixture of soy sauce, sesame oil, and cornstarch until coated.
3. Add vegetable oil to the heated skillet. Once hot, add the tofu cubes and cook until they are golden brown on all sides. Remove tofu and set aside.
4. In the same skillet, add a bit more oil if needed. Sauté garlic and ginger for a minute.
5. Add all the vegetables (bell peppers, broccoli, snap peas, carrot, mushrooms) and stir-fry for about 5-7 minutes until they are cooked but still crisp.
6. Return the tofu to the skillet and add hoisin sauce. Toss everything together until well combined and heated through.

7. Season with salt and pepper to taste.

8. Serve the vegetable stir-fry over cooked rice.

   Nutritional info: (per serving)

- Calories: 280

- Total Fat: 16g

- Saturated Fat: 2g

- Cholesterol: 0mg

- Sodium: 850mg

- Total Carbohydrate: 24g

- Dietary Fiber: 5g

- Sugars: 9g

- Protein: 15g

Butternut Squash Risotto

Preparation time: 10 minutes

Cooking time: 35 minutes

Number of servings: 6

Ingredients:

- 1 butternut squash, peeled, seeded, and diced
- 6 cups vegetable broth
- 2 tablespoons olive oil
- 1 onion, finely chopped
- 2 cups Arborio rice
- ½ cup dry white wine
- ½ cup grated Parmesan cheese
- Salt and pepper to taste
- Chopped parsley for garnish

Directions:

1. In a pot, bring the vegetable broth to a simmer.

2. In a separate large skillet or pot, heat olive oil over medium heat. Add the chopped onion and sauté until translucent.

3. Add Arborio rice to the skillet and stir for a couple of minutes until the rice is coated with oil and slightly translucent around the edges.

4. Pour in the white wine and stir until it's absorbed by the rice.

5. Begin adding the warm vegetable broth, one ladle at a time, stirring frequently and allowing the liquid to be absorbed before adding more. Continue this process for about 20-25 minutes or until the rice is creamy and cooked.

6. While cooking the risotto, steam or roast the diced butternut squash until tender.

7. Fold the cooked butternut squash into the risotto along with the Parmesan cheese. Season with salt and pepper to taste.
8. Garnish with chopped parsley before serving.

Nutritional info: (per serving)

- Calories: 320
- Total Fat: 7g
- Saturated Fat: 2g
- Cholesterol: 5mg
- Sodium: 780mg
- Total Carbohydrate: 56g
- Dietary Fiber: 5g
- Sugars: 4g
- Protein: 7g

Eggplant and Chickpea Curry

Preparation time: 20 minutes

Cooking time: 30 minutes

Number of servings: 4

Ingredients:

- 1 large eggplant, cubed
- 1 can (15 oz) chickpeas, drained and rinsed
- 2 tablespoons olive oil
- 1 onion, diced
- 3 cloves garlic, minced
- 1 tablespoon fresh ginger, grated
- 2 tomatoes, chopped
- 1 can (14 oz) coconut milk
- 2 tablespoons curry powder

- 1 teaspoon ground cumin
- 1 teaspoon ground coriander
- Salt and pepper to taste
- Fresh cilantro for garnish
- Cooked rice or naan for serving

Directions:

1. Heat olive oil in a large pan over medium heat. Add diced onion and cook until translucent.
2. Add minced garlic and grated ginger, cook for another minute.
3. Stir in the curry powder, ground cumin, and ground coriander, cooking for another minute until fragrant.
4. Add the cubed eggplant and chickpeas to the pan, stirring to coat them with the spices.

5. Pour in the chopped tomatoes and coconut milk. Stir well, bring to a simmer, and cook for 20-25 minutes or until the eggplant is tender.
6. Season with salt and pepper to taste.
7. Garnish with fresh cilantro and serve with rice or naan.

Nutritional info: (per serving)

- Calories: 320
- Total Fat: 20g
- Saturated Fat: 12g
- Cholesterol: 0mg
- Sodium: 680mg
- Total Carbohydrate: 30g
- Dietary Fiber: 9g
- Sugars: 8g

- Protein: 8g

Spinach and Ricotta Stuffed Shells

Preparation time: 25 minutes

Cooking time: 30 minutes

Number of servings: 6

Ingredients:

- 1 box (12 oz) jumbo pasta shells
- 2 cups ricotta cheese
- 2 cups chopped spinach, cooked and drained
- 1 cup shredded mozzarella cheese
- 1/2 cup grated Parmesan cheese
- 1 egg
- 2 cloves garlic, minced

- 1 teaspoon dried basil
- 1 teaspoon dried oregano
- Salt and pepper to taste
- 3 cups marinara sauce

Directions:

1. Preheat the oven to 350°F (175°C).
2. Cook the jumbo pasta shells according to package instructions until al dente. Drain and set aside.
3. In a mixing bowl, combine the ricotta cheese, chopped spinach, mozzarella cheese, Parmesan cheese, egg, minced garlic, dried basil, dried oregano, salt, and pepper.

4. Stuff each cooked pasta shell with the ricotta-spinach mixture and place them in a baking dish.

5. Pour marinara sauce over the stuffed shells, covering them evenly.

6. Cover the baking dish with foil and bake for 25 minutes.

7. Remove the foil and bake for an additional 5 minutes or until the sauce is bubbly and the cheese is melted.

8. Serve hot.

Nutritional info: (per serving)

- Calories: 380
- Total Fat: 15g
- Saturated Fat: 8g

- Cholesterol: 65mg
- Sodium: 820mg
- Total Carbohydrate: 38g
- Dietary Fiber: 4g
- Sugars: 8g
- Protein: 22g

Vegetarian Shepherd's Pie

Preparation time: 30 minutes

Cooking time: 40 minutes

Number of servings: 8

Ingredients:

- 4 large potatoes, peeled and cubed
- 2 tablespoons butter

- 1/2 cup milk

- Salt and pepper to taste

- 2 tablespoons olive oil

- 1 onion, diced

- 2 cloves garlic, minced

- 2 carrots, diced

- 1 cup green peas

- 1 cup corn kernels

- 1 can (15 oz) lentils, drained and rinsed

- 2 tablespoons tomato paste

- 1 teaspoon dried thyme

- 1 teaspoon dried rosemary

- 1 cup vegetable broth

- 1 cup shredded cheddar cheese (optional)

Directions:

1. Preheat oven to 375°F (190°C).

2. Boil the cubed potatoes in salted water until tender. Drain and mash with butter, milk, salt, and pepper. Set aside.

3. Heat olive oil in a large skillet over medium heat. Add diced onion and cook until translucent.

4. Add minced garlic, diced carrots, green peas, and corn kernels. Sauté for a few minutes.

5. Stir in the lentils, tomato paste, dried thyme, dried rosemary, and vegetable broth. Simmer for 5-7 minutes until the mixture thickens slightly.

6. Transfer the vegetable mixture to a baking dish and spread the mashed potatoes on top, covering the filling.

7. Optional: Sprinkle shredded cheddar cheese over the mashed potatoes.

8. Bake for 25-30 minutes or until the top is golden brown.

9. Let it cool for a few minutes before serving.

Nutritional info: (per serving)

- Calories: 320
- Total Fat: 8g
- Saturated Fat: 4g
- Cholesterol: 15mg
- Sodium: 480mg
- Total Carbohydrate: 50g
- Dietary Fiber: 10g
- Sugars: 6g
- Protein: 13g

Veggie Pad Thai

Preparation time: 20 minutes

Cooking time: 15 minutes

Number of servings: 4

Ingredients:

- 8 oz rice noodles
- 2 tablespoons vegetable oil
- 1 block (14 oz) firm tofu, drained and pressed, cut into cubes
- 2 cloves garlic, minced
- 1 red bell pepper, thinly sliced
- 1 carrot, julienned
- 1 cup bean sprouts

- 3 green onions, chopped
- 1/4 cup chopped peanuts
- Lime wedges for garnish

For the Sauce:

- 3 tablespoons soy sauce
- 2 tablespoons tamarind paste
- 2 tablespoons brown sugar
- 1 tablespoon rice vinegar
- 1 teaspoon sriracha sauce (adjust to taste)

Directions:

1. Cook the rice noodles according to package instructions. Drain and set aside.
2. In a small bowl, whisk together the ingredients for the sauce - soy sauce, tamarind paste,

brown sugar, rice vinegar, and sriracha sauce. Set aside.

3. Heat vegetable oil in a large skillet or wok over medium-high heat. Add tofu cubes and cook until golden brown. Remove from the skillet and set aside.

4. In the same skillet, add a bit more oil if needed. Sauté minced garlic until fragrant.

5. Add sliced bell pepper, julienned carrot, and bean sprouts. Stir-fry for a few minutes until the vegetables are tender-crisp.

6. Add the cooked noodles, tofu, and the prepared sauce to the skillet. Toss everything together until well combined and heated through.

7. Serve the veggie pad Thai topped with chopped green onions, chopped peanuts, and lime wedges for garnish.

   Nutritional info: (per serving)

- Calories: 420
- Total Fat: 16g
- Saturated Fat: 2g
- Cholesterol: 0mg
- Sodium: 880mg
- Total Carbohydrate: 58g
- Dietary Fiber: 5g
- Sugars: 9g
- Protein: 15g

Lentil Stew

Preparation time: 15 minutes

Cooking time: 40 minutes

Number of servings: 6

Ingredients:

- 1 cup dried lentils, rinsed
- 4 cups vegetable broth
- 2 tablespoons olive oil
- 1 onion, chopped
- 3 cloves garlic, minced
- 2 carrots, diced
- 2 celery stalks, diced
- 1 can (14 oz) diced tomatoes
- 1 teaspoon dried thyme
- 1 teaspoon paprika

- Salt and pepper to taste

- Fresh parsley for garnish

Directions:

1. In a pot, combine lentils and vegetable broth. Bring to a boil, then reduce heat and simmer for 20-25 minutes or until lentils are tender.

2. In a separate skillet, heat olive oil over medium heat. Add chopped onion and cook until translucent.

3. Add minced garlic, diced carrots, and diced celery to the skillet. Sauté for a few minutes until the vegetables are slightly tender.

4. Stir in the diced tomatoes, dried thyme, paprika, salt, and pepper.

5. Combine the vegetable mixture with the cooked lentils and broth. Simmer for an additional 10-15 minutes.
6. Adjust seasoning if needed and serve hot, garnished with fresh parsley.

Nutritional info: (per serving)

- Calories: 220
- Total Fat: 5g
- Saturated Fat: 1g
- Cholesterol: 0mg
- Sodium: 780mg
- Total Carbohydrate: 33g
- Dietary Fiber: 14g
- Sugars: 5g
- Protein: 12g

Roasted Vegetable Pasta

Preparation time: 15 minutes

Cooking time: 30 minutes

Number of servings: 4

Ingredients:

- 8 oz pasta of your choice
- 2 cups assorted vegetables (bell peppers, zucchini, cherry tomatoes, etc.), chopped
- 3 tablespoons olive oil
- 3 cloves garlic, minced
- 1 teaspoon dried basil
- 1 teaspoon dried oregano
- Salt and pepper to taste

- Grated Parmesan cheese for garnish
- Fresh basil leaves for garnish

Directions:

1. Preheat oven to 400°F (200°C).
2. Toss chopped vegetables with 2 tablespoons of olive oil, minced garlic, dried basil, dried oregano, salt, and pepper on a baking sheet.
3. Roast the vegetables in the preheated oven for 20-25 minutes or until they are tender and slightly caramelized.
4. Cook pasta according to package instructions. Drain and set aside.
5. In a skillet, heat the remaining tablespoon of olive oil over medium heat. Add the roasted vegetables and cooked pasta to the skillet. Toss to combine and heat through.

6. Season with additional salt and pepper if needed.
7. Serve hot, garnished with grated Parmesan cheese and fresh basil leaves.

   Nutritional info: (per serving)

- Calories: 380
- Total Fat: 12g
- Saturated Fat: 2g
- Cholesterol: 0mg
- Sodium: 240mg
- Total Carbohydrate: 58g
- Dietary Fiber: 5g
- Sugars: 4g
- Protein: 10g

Quinoa and Black Bean Stuffed Bell Peppers

Preparation time: 20 minutes

Cooking time: 35 minutes

Number of servings: 4

Ingredients:

- 4 large bell peppers, halved and seeds removed
- 1 cup quinoa, rinsed
- 2 cups vegetable broth
- 1 can (15 oz) black beans, drained and rinsed
- 1 cup corn kernels
- 1 onion, diced
- 2 cloves garlic, minced
- 1 teaspoon ground cumin

- 1 teaspoon chili powder
- Salt and pepper to taste
- 1 cup shredded cheddar cheese (optional)
- Chopped fresh cilantro for garnish

Directions:

1. Preheat oven to 375°F (190°C).
2. In a pot, combine quinoa and vegetable broth. Bring to a boil, then reduce heat, cover, and simmer for 15-20 minutes until quinoa is cooked and liquid is absorbed.
3. In a skillet, heat olive oil over medium heat. Sauté diced onion and minced garlic until softened.
4. Add black beans, corn kernels, ground cumin, chili powder, salt, and pepper to the skillet. Stir

and cook for a few minutes until heated through.

5. Combine the cooked quinoa with the bean and corn mixture.

6. Stuff each halved bell pepper with the quinoa and bean mixture.

7. Place stuffed peppers in a baking dish. If desired, sprinkle shredded cheddar cheese on top.

8. Bake in the preheated oven for 20-25 minutes or until peppers are tender.

9. Garnish with chopped fresh cilantro before serving.

Nutritional info: (per serving)

- Calories: 320
- Total Fat: 6g

- Saturated Fat: 3g
- Cholesterol: 15mg
- Sodium: 580mg
- Total Carbohydrate: 53g
- Dietary Fiber: 11g
- Sugars: 8g
- Protein: 14g

Caprese Pasta Salad

Preparation time: 15 minutes

Cooking time: 10 minutes

Number of servings: 4

Ingredients:

- 8 oz pasta (penne or fusilli work well)

- 1 cup cherry tomatoes, halved
- 1 cup fresh mozzarella cheese, diced
- 1/4 cup fresh basil leaves, chopped
- 3 tablespoons extra-virgin olive oil
- 2 tablespoons balsamic vinegar
- Salt and pepper to taste

Directions:

1. Cook the pasta according to package instructions. Drain and let it cool.
2. In a large mixing bowl, combine the cooked pasta, halved cherry tomatoes, diced mozzarella cheese, and chopped basil.
3. Drizzle olive oil and balsamic vinegar over the salad. Toss gently to coat everything evenly.
4. Season with salt and pepper to taste.

5. Serve immediately or refrigerate until ready to serve.

   Nutritional info: (per serving)

- Calories: 380
- Total Fat: 18g
- Saturated Fat: 6g
- Cholesterol: 25mg
- Sodium: 250mg
- Total Carbohydrate: 40g
- Dietary Fiber: 2g
- Sugars: 3g
- Protein: 15g

Mushroom Bourguignon

Preparation time: 15 minutes

Cooking time: 40 minutes

Number of servings: 4

Ingredients:

- 2 tablespoons olive oil
- 1 onion, diced
- 3 cloves garlic, minced
- 12 oz mushrooms, sliced (use a mix like cremini and button)
- 2 carrots, sliced
- 2 tablespoons tomato paste
- 1 cup vegetable broth
- 1 cup red wine (like a Burgundy or Pinot Noir)
- 1 teaspoon dried thyme

- Salt and pepper to taste
- Chopped fresh parsley for garnish

Directions:

1. Heat olive oil in a large skillet over medium heat. Add diced onion and cook until translucent.
2. Add minced garlic and sliced mushrooms. Sauté until the mushrooms begin to brown.
3. Stir in sliced carrots and tomato paste, cooking for a couple of minutes.
4. Pour in the vegetable broth and red wine. Add dried thyme, salt, and pepper.
5. Simmer uncovered for 25-30 minutes or until the sauce thickens and the carrots are tender.
6. Adjust seasoning if needed. Garnish with chopped fresh parsley before serving.

7. Serve hot over mashed potatoes, rice, or pasta.

   Nutritional info: (per serving)

- Calories: 180
- Total Fat: 7g
- Saturated Fat: 1g
- Cholesterol: 0mg
- Sodium: 280mg
- Total Carbohydrate: 16g
- Dietary Fiber: 4g
- Sugars: 7g
- Protein: 4g

Ratatouille Tart

Preparation time: 30 minutes

Cooking time: 40 minutes

Number of servings: 6

Ingredients:

- 1 pre-made pie crust or homemade pie dough
- 1 eggplant, thinly sliced
- 2 zucchinis, thinly sliced
- 2 tomatoes, thinly sliced
- 1 onion, thinly sliced
- 2 cloves garlic, minced
- 3 tablespoons olive oil
- 1 teaspoon dried thyme
- Salt and pepper to taste
- 1/2 cup shredded mozzarella cheese (optional)
- Fresh basil leaves for garnish

Directions:

1. Preheat oven to 375°F (190°C).

2. Roll out the pie crust and place it in a tart pan. Prick the bottom with a fork and bake for 10 minutes. Remove from oven and set aside.

3. In a skillet, heat olive oil over medium heat. Sauté minced garlic and sliced onion until softened.

4. Layer the thinly sliced eggplant, zucchini, tomatoes, and onion-garlic mixture in the pre-baked pie crust, arranging them in an overlapping pattern.

5. Drizzle with a little more olive oil, sprinkle dried thyme, salt, and pepper on top.

6. Optional: Sprinkle shredded mozzarella cheese over the vegetables.

7. Bake in the preheated oven for 30-35 minutes or until the vegetables are tender and the crust is golden brown.
8. Garnish with fresh basil leaves before serving.

Nutritional info: (per serving)

- Calories: 280
- Total Fat: 17g
- Saturated Fat: 4g
- Cholesterol: 20mg
- Sodium: 250mg
- Total Carbohydrate: 27g
- Dietary Fiber: 5g
- Sugars: 5g
- Protein: 6g

Sweet Potato and Black Bean Enchiladas

Preparation time: 30 minutes

Cooking time: 30 minutes

Number of servings: 4

Ingredients:

- 2 large sweet potatoes, peeled and cubed
- 1 can (15 oz) black beans, drained and rinsed
- 1 cup corn kernels (fresh, frozen, or canned)
- 1 red bell pepper, diced
- 1 onion, diced
- 2 cloves garlic, minced
- 1 tablespoon chili powder
- 1 teaspoon ground cumin
- Salt and pepper to taste

- 8-10 small flour tortillas

- 2 cups enchilada sauce

- 1 cup shredded cheddar cheese (or cheese of choice)

- Chopped fresh cilantro for garnish

Directions:

1. Preheat oven to 375°F (190°C).

2. Boil or steam the sweet potato cubes until tender. Mash them in a bowl and set aside.

3. In a skillet, sauté diced onion and minced garlic until softened.

4. Add diced red bell pepper, black beans, and corn kernels to the skillet. Cook for a few minutes.

5. Stir in chili powder, ground cumin, salt, and pepper. Cook for an additional 5 minutes.
6. Spread a spoonful of the mashed sweet potatoes onto each tortilla. Add the bean and vegetable mixture on top.
7. Roll up the tortillas and place them seam-side down in a baking dish.
8. Pour enchilada sauce over the rolled tortillas. Sprinkle shredded cheese on top.
9. Bake in the preheated oven for 20-25 minutes or until the cheese is melted and bubbly.
10. Garnish with chopped fresh cilantro before serving.

Nutritional info: (per serving)

- Calories: 480
- Total Fat: 14g

- Saturated Fat: 6g

- Cholesterol: 25mg

- Sodium: 1150mg

- Total Carbohydrate: 74g

- Dietary Fiber: 13g

- Sugars: 13g

- Protein: 18g

Spinach and Feta Stuffed Mushrooms

Preparation time: 20 minutes

Cooking time: 20 minutes

Number of servings: 4

Ingredients:

- 12 large button mushrooms, stems removed and chopped
- 2 cups fresh spinach, chopped
- 1/2 cup crumbled feta cheese
- 2 cloves garlic, minced
- 2 tablespoons olive oil
- Salt and pepper to taste
- 2 tablespoons grated Parmesan cheese
- Chopped fresh parsley for garnish

Directions:

1. Preheat oven to 375°F (190°C).
2. Heat olive oil in a skillet over medium heat. Sauté chopped mushroom stems and minced garlic until softened.

3. Add chopped spinach to the skillet and cook until wilted. Remove from heat.

4. In a mixing bowl, combine the sautéed mixture with crumbled feta cheese. Season with salt and pepper.

5. Place the mushroom caps on a baking sheet. Stuff each mushroom cap with the spinach and feta mixture.

6. Sprinkle grated Parmesan cheese over the stuffed mushrooms.

7. Bake in the preheated oven for 15-20 minutes or until the mushrooms are tender and the cheese is golden.

8. Garnish with chopped fresh parsley before serving.

Nutritional info: (per serving)

- Calories: 140

- Total Fat: 10g

- Saturated Fat: 3g

- Cholesterol: 15mg

- Sodium: 290mg

- Total Carbohydrate: 7g

- Dietary Fiber: 2g

- Sugars: 2g

- Protein: 6g

Tomato and Basil Pizza

Preparation time: 20 minutes

Cooking time: 15 minutes

Number of servings: 4

Ingredients:

- 1 pre-made pizza dough or homemade dough
- 1/2 cup pizza sauce or marinara sauce
- 2 tomatoes, thinly sliced
- 1 cup shredded mozzarella cheese
- Fresh basil leaves, torn
- Olive oil for drizzling
- Salt and pepper to taste
- Red pepper flakes (optional)

Directions:

1. Preheat oven to 450°F (230°C).
2. Roll out the pizza dough on a floured surface and place it on a baking sheet or pizza pan.
3. Spread pizza sauce evenly over the dough.

4. Arrange the thinly sliced tomatoes on top of the sauce.

5. Sprinkle shredded mozzarella cheese over the tomatoes.

6. Season with salt and pepper. Drizzle a little olive oil over the pizza.

7. Bake in the preheated oven for 12-15 minutes or until the crust is golden and the cheese is bubbly.

8. Remove from the oven, garnish with torn fresh basil leaves and red pepper flakes if desired.

9. Slice and serve hot.

    Nutritional info: (per serving)

- Calories: 320
- Total Fat: 11g

- Saturated Fat: 4g
- Cholesterol: 20mg
- Sodium: 620mg
- Total Carbohydrate: 45g
- Dietary Fiber: 3g
- Sugars: 4g
- Protein: 11g

Baked Eggplant Parmesan

Preparation time: 30 minutes

Cooking time: 45 minutes

Number of servings: 4

Ingredients:

- 2 medium eggplants, sliced into rounds

- 2 cups marinara sauce
- 2 cups breadcrumbs
- 1 cup grated Parmesan cheese
- 2 eggs, beaten
- 1 teaspoon dried oregano
- 1 teaspoon dried basil
- Salt and pepper to taste
- Olive oil for brushing

Directions:

1. Preheat oven to 400°F (200°C).
2. Arrange eggplant slices on a baking sheet. Brush both sides of the slices with olive oil and sprinkle with salt and pepper.
3. Bake the eggplant slices for 15-20 minutes or until they are tender.

4. In a shallow dish, mix breadcrumbs, grated Parmesan cheese, dried oregano, dried basil, salt, and pepper.

5. Dip each baked eggplant slice into beaten eggs, then coat with the breadcrumb mixture.

6. In a baking dish, spread a thin layer of marinara sauce. Place the breaded eggplant slices in the dish, slightly overlapping.

7. Top the eggplant slices with more marinara sauce and grated Parmesan cheese.

8. Bake in the preheated oven for 20-25 minutes or until the cheese is golden and bubbly.

9. Serve hot, garnished with fresh basil if desired. Nutritional info: (per serving)

- Calories: 320
- Total Fat: 10g

- Saturated Fat: 4g

- Cholesterol: 95mg

- Sodium: 820mg

- Total Carbohydrate: 41g

- Dietary Fiber: 8g

- Sugars: 11g

- Protein: 17g

Veggie Fajitas

Preparation time: 20 minutes

Cooking time: 15 minutes

Number of servings: 4

Ingredients:

- 2 bell peppers (any color), sliced

- 1 onion, sliced
- 1 zucchini, sliced
- 1 yellow squash, sliced
- 1 tablespoon olive oil
- 2 teaspoons chili powder
- 1 teaspoon cumin
- 1 teaspoon paprika
- Salt and pepper to taste
- 8 small flour tortillas
- Optional toppings: shredded cheese, salsa, guacamole, sour cream

Directions:

1. Heat olive oil in a large skillet over medium-high heat.

2. Add sliced bell peppers, onion, zucchini, and yellow squash to the skillet.
3. Sprinkle chili powder, cumin, paprika, salt, and pepper over the vegetables. Stir to coat evenly.
4. Cook for 8-10 minutes, stirring occasionally, until the vegetables are tender-crisp.
5. Warm the flour tortillas in a separate skillet or microwave.
6. Spoon the cooked vegetable mixture onto the warm tortillas.
7. Add optional toppings like shredded cheese, salsa, guacamole, or sour cream if desired.
8. Serve hot.

Nutritional info: (per serving)

- Calories: 280
- Total Fat: 7g

- Saturated Fat: 1g
- Cholesterol: 0mg
- Sodium: 460mg
- Total Carbohydrate: 49g
- Dietary Fiber: 7g
- Sugars: 7g
- Protein: 8g

Creamy Pumpkin and Sage Pasta

Preparation time: 15 minutes

Cooking time: 20 minutes

Number of servings: 4

Ingredients:

- 8 oz pasta of your choice

- 2 tablespoons butter
- 2 cloves garlic, minced
- 1/4 cup fresh sage leaves, chopped
- 1 cup pumpkin puree
- 1 cup vegetable broth
- 1/2 cup heavy cream
- 1/4 cup grated Parmesan cheese
- Salt and pepper to taste
- Crushed red pepper flakes for garnish (optional)

Directions:

1. Cook pasta according to package instructions. Drain and set aside.

2. In a skillet, melt butter over medium heat. Add minced garlic and chopped sage leaves. Cook for a minute until fragrant.
3. Stir in pumpkin puree and vegetable broth. Simmer for 5 minutes.
4. Reduce heat to low. Add heavy cream and grated Parmesan cheese. Stir until the sauce is smooth and heated through.
5. Season with salt and pepper to taste.
6. Add the cooked pasta to the skillet and toss until well coated with the pumpkin sauce.
7. Serve hot, garnished with crushed red pepper flakes if desired.

Nutritional info: (per serving)

- Calories: 390
- Total Fat: 17g

- Saturated Fat: 10g
- Cholesterol: 50mg
- Sodium: 320mg
- Total Carbohydrate: 49g
- Dietary Fiber: 5g
- Sugars: 4g
- Protein: 9g

Chickpea Tikka Masala

Preparation time: 15 minutes

Cooking time: 30 minutes

Number of servings: 4

Ingredients:

- 2 cans (15 oz each) chickpeas, drained and rinsed
- 1 onion, finely chopped
- 3 cloves garlic, minced
- 1 tablespoon ginger, grated
- 2 tablespoons tomato paste
- 1 can (14 oz) diced tomatoes
- 1 cup vegetable broth
- 1 cup coconut milk
- 2 tablespoons olive oil
- 2 teaspoons garam masala
- 1 teaspoon ground cumin
- 1 teaspoon ground coriander
- 1/2 teaspoon turmeric
- 1/2 teaspoon paprika

- Salt and pepper to taste
- Fresh cilantro for garnish
- Cooked rice or naan for serving

Directions:

1. Heat olive oil in a large skillet over medium heat. Add chopped onion and cook until softened.
2. Add minced garlic and grated ginger to the skillet. Sauté for a minute until fragrant.
3. Stir in garam masala, ground cumin, ground coriander, turmeric, and paprika. Cook for a minute to toast the spices.
4. Add tomato paste and diced tomatoes to the skillet. Cook for a couple of minutes.

5. Pour in vegetable broth and coconut milk. Stir to combine.
6. Add drained and rinsed chickpeas to the skillet. Simmer for 15-20 minutes, stirring occasionally, until the sauce thickens slightly.
7. Season with salt and pepper to taste.
8. Serve the chickpea tikka masala over cooked rice or with naan. Garnish with fresh cilantro. Nutritional info: (per serving, excluding rice or naan)

- Calories: 380
- Total Fat: 18g
- Saturated Fat: 9g
- Cholesterol: 0mg
- Sodium: 760mg

- Total Carbohydrate: 46g
- Dietary Fiber: 11g
- Sugars: 11g
- Protein: 12g

Zucchini Noodles with Pesto

Preparation time: 15 minutes

Cooking time: 5 minutes

Number of servings: 2

Ingredients:

- 4 medium zucchinis
- 1/2 cup fresh basil leaves

- 1/4 cup pine nuts or walnuts
- 2 cloves garlic
- 1/4 cup grated Parmesan cheese
- 1/4 cup olive oil
- Salt and pepper to taste
- Cherry tomatoes (optional, for garnish)
- Extra grated Parmesan (optional, for garnish)

Directions:

1. Using a spiralizer or a vegetable peeler, create zucchini noodles (zoodles) from the zucchinis. Set aside.
2. In a food processor, combine fresh basil leaves, pine nuts or walnuts, garlic, grated Parmesan cheese, and olive oil. Pulse until a smooth pesto consistency is achieved.

3. Heat a skillet over medium heat. Add the zucchini noodles and cook for 2-3 minutes, tossing gently, until they are just slightly softened.
4. Remove the skillet from heat and toss the zucchini noodles with the prepared pesto until well coated.
5. Season with salt and pepper to taste.
6. Optionally, garnish with halved cherry tomatoes and extra grated Parmesan before serving.

Nutritional info: (per serving)

- Calories: 320
- Total Fat: 28g
- Saturated Fat: 5g

- Cholesterol: 8mg

- Sodium: 250mg

- Total Carbohydrate: 12g

- Dietary Fiber: 4g

- Sugars: 6g

- Protein: 8g

Stuffed Acorn Squash

Preparation time: 20 minutes

Cooking time: 50 minutes

Number of servings: 4

Ingredients:

- 2 acorn squashes, halved and seeds removed

- 1 cup quinoa, rinsed

- 2 cups vegetable broth
- 1 tablespoon olive oil
- 1 onion, diced
- 2 cloves garlic, minced
- 1 bell pepper, diced
- 1 cup cooked black beans
- 1 teaspoon ground cumin
- 1 teaspoon smoked paprika
- Salt and pepper to taste
- Chopped fresh parsley for garnish

Directions:

1. Preheat oven to 400°F (200°C).
2. Place the halved acorn squashes on a baking sheet, cut side down. Bake for 30-35 minutes or until tender.

3. In a pot, combine quinoa and vegetable broth. Bring to a boil, then reduce heat, cover, and simmer for 15-20 minutes until quinoa is cooked.
4. Heat olive oil in a skillet over medium heat. Sauté diced onion, minced garlic, and diced bell pepper until softened.
5. Add cooked quinoa, black beans, ground cumin, smoked paprika, salt, and pepper to the skillet. Mix well and cook for a few minutes.
6. Remove the baked squash halves from the oven and carefully flip them over.
7. Fill each squash half with the quinoa and black bean mixture.
8. Return the stuffed squash to the oven and bake for an additional 15 minutes.

9. Garnish with chopped fresh parsley before serving.

Nutritional info: (per serving)

- Calories: 320
- Total Fat: 6g
- Saturated Fat: 1g
- Cholesterol: 0mg
- Sodium: 480mg
- Total Carbohydrate: 60g
- Dietary Fiber: 12g
- Sugars: 5g
- Protein: 11g

Veggie Curry with Cauliflower Rice

Preparation time: 15 minutes

Cooking time: 25 minutes

Number of servings: 4

Ingredients:

- 1 tablespoon olive oil
- 1 onion, diced
- 3 cloves garlic, minced
- 2 carrots, sliced
- 1 bell pepper, chopped
- 1 zucchini, diced
- 1 cup broccoli florets
- 1 can (14 oz) chickpeas, drained and rinsed
- 1 can (14 oz) coconut milk
- 2 tablespoons red curry paste

- 1 teaspoon ground turmeric
- Salt and pepper to taste
- Fresh cilantro for garnish
- 1 head cauliflower, grated (for cauliflower rice)

Directions:

1. Heat olive oil in a large skillet or wok over medium heat. Add diced onion and minced garlic. Cook until onions are translucent.
2. Add sliced carrots, chopped bell pepper, diced zucchini, and broccoli florets to the skillet. Sauté for a few minutes until slightly tender.
3. Stir in drained chickpeas, coconut milk, red curry paste, and ground turmeric. Simmer for 10-15 minutes, stirring occasionally.

4. While the curry is simmering, prepare the cauliflower rice by pulsing the cauliflower florets in a food processor until they resemble rice grains. Steam or sauté in a separate pan until tender.
5. Season the curry with salt and pepper to taste.
6. Serve the veggie curry over cauliflower rice and garnish with fresh cilantro.

    Nutritional info: (per serving, including cauliflower rice)

- Calories: 280
- Total Fat: 15g
- Saturated Fat: 11g
- Cholesterol: 0mg
- Sodium: 320mg

- Total Carbohydrate: 30g
- Dietary Fiber: 10g
- Sugars: 9g
- Protein: 9g

Portobello Mushroom Burgers

Preparation time: 15 minutes

Cooking time: 15 minutes

Number of servings: 4

Ingredients:

- 4 large portobello mushroom caps
- 2 tablespoons balsamic vinegar
- 2 tablespoons olive oil
- 2 cloves garlic, minced

- 1 teaspoon dried thyme
- Salt and pepper to taste
- 4 whole grain burger buns
- Lettuce, tomato slices, avocado (optional, for topping)
- Your favorite burger condiments

Directions:

1. Clean the portobello mushroom caps and remove the stems.
2. In a shallow dish, whisk together balsamic vinegar, olive oil, minced garlic, dried thyme, salt, and pepper.
3. Marinate the mushroom caps in the mixture for 10-15 minutes, turning occasionally to coat.

4. Preheat grill or grill pan over medium-high heat. Grill the mushroom caps for 5-7 minutes on each side until tender.

5. Toast the whole grain burger buns on the grill for a minute or until lightly browned.

6. Assemble the burgers by placing grilled portobello mushroom caps on the bottom bun. Add lettuce, tomato slices, avocado, and any desired toppings.

7. Spread condiments on the top bun, place on top of the toppings, and serve.

   Nutritional info: (per serving, without additional toppings)

- Calories: 230
- Total Fat: 9g

- Saturated Fat: 1g
- Cholesterol: 0mg
- Sodium: 350mg
- Total Carbohydrate: 30g
- Dietary Fiber: 4g
- Sugars: 5g
- Protein: 7g

Veggie Jambalaya

Preparation time: 20 minutes

Cooking time: 35 minutes

Number of servings: 6

Ingredients:

- 1 tablespoon olive oil

- 1 onion, diced
- 3 cloves garlic, minced
- 1 bell pepper, diced
- 2 celery stalks, chopped
- 1 cup okra, sliced
- 1 can (14 oz) diced tomatoes
- 1 cup vegetable broth
- 1 cup long-grain white rice
- 1 teaspoon smoked paprika
- 1 teaspoon dried thyme
- 1/2 teaspoon cayenne pepper (adjust to taste)
- Salt and pepper to taste
- 1 cup cooked kidney beans
- Chopped green onions for garnish

Directions:

1. Heat olive oil in a large skillet or pot over medium heat. Add diced onion and minced garlic. Sauté until onions are translucent.
2. Add diced bell pepper, chopped celery, and sliced okra to the skillet. Cook for a few minutes until slightly tender.
3. Stir in diced tomatoes, vegetable broth, long-grain white rice, smoked paprika, dried thyme, cayenne pepper, salt, and pepper.
4. Bring the mixture to a boil, then reduce heat to low. Cover and simmer for 20-25 minutes or until the rice is cooked and the liquid is absorbed.
5. Fold in cooked kidney beans and cook for an additional 5 minutes to heat through.

6. Adjust seasoning if needed. Garnish with chopped green onions before serving.

   Nutritional info: (per serving)

- Calories: 240
- Total Fat: 3g
- Saturated Fat: 0g
- Cholesterol: 0mg
- Sodium: 480mg
- Total Carbohydrate: 47g
- Dietary Fiber: 6g
- Sugars: 5g
- Protein: 7g

Baked Stuffed Tomatoes

Preparation time: 15 minutes

Cooking time: 25 minutes

Number of servings: 4

Ingredients:

- 4 large beefsteak or Roma tomatoes
- 1 cup breadcrumbs (Panko or homemade)
- 1/2 cup grated Parmesan cheese
- 2 cloves garlic, minced
- 1/4 cup fresh basil, chopped
- 2 tablespoons olive oil
- Salt and pepper to taste
- Fresh parsley for garnish

Directions:

1. Preheat oven to 375°F (190°C).

2. Slice off the top of each tomato and gently scoop out the pulp and seeds, leaving the tomato shell intact. Reserve the pulp in a bowl.
3. In a separate bowl, mix breadcrumbs, grated Parmesan cheese, minced garlic, chopped basil, olive oil, salt, and pepper. Combine well.
4. Chop the reserved tomato pulp and add it to the breadcrumb mixture. Stir until everything is evenly mixed.
5. Stuff each hollowed-out tomato with the breadcrumb mixture, pressing gently to pack it in.
6. Place the stuffed tomatoes on a baking dish or sheet. Drizzle a little olive oil over the tops if desired.

7. Bake in the preheated oven for 20-25 minutes or until the tomatoes are tender and the breadcrumb topping is golden brown.
8. Garnish with fresh parsley before serving.

Nutritional info: (per serving)

- Calories: 180
- Total Fat: 9g
- Saturated Fat: 2g
- Cholesterol: 5mg
- Sodium: 280mg
- Total Carbohydrate: 19g
- Dietary Fiber: 3g
- Sugars: 5g
- Protein: 6g

Chapter 7

Snacks and Appetizers

Guacamole with Tortilla Chips

Preparation time: 15 minutes

Cooking time: 0 minutes

Number of servings: 4

Ingredients:

- 3 ripe avocados
- 1 lime, juiced
- 1/2 teaspoon salt
- 1/2 teaspoon ground cumin

- 1/2 teaspoon cayenne pepper
- 1/2 medium onion, diced
- 2 Roma tomatoes, diced
- 3 tablespoons chopped fresh cilantro
- 2 cloves garlic, minced
- Tortilla chips for serving

Directions:

1. Cut the avocados in half, remove the pits, and scoop the flesh into a mixing bowl.
2. Mash the avocado with a fork until it's chunky or smooth, depending on your preference.
3. Add lime juice, salt, cumin, and cayenne pepper. Mix well.
4. Fold in the diced onion, tomatoes, cilantro, and minced garlic.

5. Taste and adjust seasoning if needed.

6. Serve immediately with tortilla chips.

   Nutritional info: (per serving)

- Calories: 240
- Fat: 20g
- Carbohydrates: 15g
- Protein: 3g

Caprese Skewers

Preparation time: 15 minutes

Cooking time: 0 minutes

Number of servings: 6

Ingredients:

- Fresh mozzarella balls
- Cherry tomatoes
- Fresh basil leaves
- Balsamic glaze
- Skewers

Directions:

1. Thread a mozzarella ball, a cherry tomato, and a basil leaf onto each skewer, repeating until the skewer is filled.
2. Arrange the skewers on a serving platter.
3. Drizzle balsamic glaze over the skewers just before serving.

Nutritional info: (per serving)

- Calories: 70
- Fat: 4g

- Carbohydrates: 3g

- Protein: 5g

Hummus with Pita Bread

Preparation time: 10 minutes

Cooking time: 0 minutes

Number of servings: 8

Ingredients:

- 2 cans (15 ounces each) chickpeas, drained and rinsed
- 1/3 cup tahini
- 2 cloves garlic, minced
- 2 tablespoons lemon juice
- 1/4 cup extra virgin olive oil

- Salt to taste
- Pita bread for serving

Directions:

1. In a food processor, blend the chickpeas, tahini, garlic, lemon juice, and olive oil until smooth.
2. Season with salt to taste and blend again.
3. If the hummus is too thick, add a little water or more olive oil until it reaches your desired consistency.
4. Transfer the hummus to a serving bowl.
5. Drizzle a little extra olive oil on top and sprinkle with paprika or chopped parsley if desired.
6. Serve with pita bread.

Nutritional info: (per serving)

- Calories: 200

- Fat: 12g

- Carbohydrates: 18g

- Protein: 7g

Veggie Spring Rolls

Preparation time: 30 minutes

Cooking time: 10 minutes

Number of servings: 8 rolls

Ingredients:

- 8 spring roll rice paper wrappers

- 1 cup shredded lettuce

- 1 cup julienned carrots

- 1 cup julienned cucumber

- 1 cup cooked vermicelli noodles
- 1/2 cup fresh mint leaves
- 1/2 cup fresh cilantro leaves
- Hoisin sauce or peanut dipping sauce

Directions:

1. Prepare a shallow dish of warm water. Dip one rice paper wrapper into the water for a few seconds until it softens.
2. Lay the wrapper flat on a clean surface.
3. Place a small amount of shredded lettuce, carrots, cucumber, noodles, mint leaves, and cilantro in the center of the wrapper.
4. Fold the sides of the wrapper inward, then roll up tightly from the bottom to form a spring roll.

5. Repeat with the remaining ingredients.
6. Serve the spring rolls with hoisin sauce or peanut dipping sauce.

    Nutritional info: (per serving, 1 roll)

- Calories: 90
- Fat: 0.5g
- Carbohydrates: 20g
- Protein: 2g

Bruschetta

Preparation time: 15 minutes

Cooking time: 10 minutes

Number of servings: 6

Ingredients:

- 6 ripe Roma tomatoes, diced
- 1/4 cup fresh basil leaves, chopped
- 2 cloves garlic, minced
- 2 tablespoons balsamic vinegar
- 2 tablespoons extra virgin olive oil
- Salt and pepper to taste
- 1 French baguette, sliced and toasted

Directions:

1. In a bowl, mix together the diced tomatoes, chopped basil, minced garlic, balsamic vinegar, olive oil, salt, and pepper.
2. Let the mixture sit for 10 minutes to allow the flavors to meld.
3. Spoon the tomato mixture onto the toasted baguette slices.

4. Serve immediately.

   Nutritional info: (per serving, 2 slices)

- Calories: 160
- Fat: 6g
- Carbohydrates: 22g
- Protein: 4g

Spinach and Artichoke Dip

Preparation time: 15 minutes

Cooking time: 25 minutes

Number of servings: 8

Ingredients:

- 1 (10-ounce) package frozen chopped spinach, thawed and drained
- 1 (14-ounce) can artichoke hearts, drained and chopped
- 1 cup grated Parmesan cheese
- 1 cup shredded mozzarella cheese
- 1 cup sour cream
- 1/2 cup mayonnaise
- 2 cloves garlic, minced
- Salt and pepper to taste
- Tortilla chips or sliced baguette for serving

Directions:

1. Preheat oven to 350°F (175°C).
2. In a mixing bowl, combine the chopped spinach, chopped artichoke hearts, Parmesan

cheese, mozzarella cheese, sour cream, mayonnaise, minced garlic, salt, and pepper.

3. Spread the mixture into a baking dish.
4. Bake for 25 minutes or until the top is golden and bubbly.
5. Serve warm with tortilla chips or sliced baguette.

Nutritional info: (per serving, 1/8 of recipe)

- Calories: 250
- Fat: 20g
- Carbohydrates: 8g
- Protein: 9g

Stuffed Mini Peppers

Preparation time: 20 minutes

Cooking time: 15 minutes

Number of servings: 6

Ingredients:

- 12 mini sweet peppers, halved and seeds removed
- 1 cup cooked quinoa
- 1/2 cup black beans, rinsed and drained
- 1/2 cup corn kernels
- 1/2 cup diced tomatoes
- 1/4 cup chopped cilantro
- 1 teaspoon chili powder
- 1/2 teaspoon cumin
- Salt and pepper to taste
- Shredded cheese for topping (optional)

Directions:

1. Preheat oven to 375°F (190°C).
2. In a bowl, mix together the cooked quinoa, black beans, corn, diced tomatoes, cilantro, chili powder, cumin, salt, and pepper.
3. Stuff each mini pepper half with the quinoa mixture.
4. Place the stuffed peppers on a baking sheet and bake for 15 minutes.
5. If desired, sprinkle shredded cheese on top of the peppers and return to the oven for an additional 5 minutes or until the cheese is melted and bubbly.
6. Serve warm.

   Nutritional info: (per serving, 4 stuffed pepper halves)

- Calories: 180
- Fat: 2g
- Carbohydrates: 35g
- Protein: 8g

Roasted Chickpeas

Preparation time: 5 minutes

Cooking time: 40 minutes

Number of servings: 4

Ingredients:

- 2 cans (15 ounces each) chickpeas, drained, rinsed, and patted dry
- 2 tablespoons olive oil
- 1 teaspoon ground cumin

- 1 teaspoon paprika

- 1/2 teaspoon garlic powder

- Salt and pepper to taste

Directions:

1. Preheat oven to 400°F (200°C).
2. In a bowl, toss the chickpeas with olive oil, ground cumin, paprika, garlic powder, salt, and pepper until evenly coated.
3. Spread the chickpeas in a single layer on a baking sheet.
4. Roast for 30-40 minutes, shaking the pan occasionally, until the chickpeas are crispy and golden brown.
5. Let them cool slightly before serving.

    Nutritional info: (per serving, 1/4 of recipe)

- Calories: 250
- Fat: 10g
- Carbohydrates: 32g
- Protein: 10g

Cheese and Crackers Platter

Preparation time: 10 minutes

Cooking time: 0 minutes

Number of servings: 6

Ingredients:

- Assorted cheeses (cheddar, brie, gouda, etc.), sliced or cubed
- Assorted crackers
- Grapes or apple slices

- Nuts (almonds, walnuts, etc.)
- Honey or jam for drizzling (optional)

Directions:

1. Arrange the assorted cheeses, crackers, grapes or apple slices, and nuts on a serving platter.
2. If desired, drizzle honey or serve jam alongside the cheeses for added flavor.
3. Serve the cheese and crackers platter immediately.

Nutritional info: (approximate, varies based on selection)

- Calories: Varies
- Fat: Varies
- Carbohydrates: Varies
- Protein: Varies

Greek Yogurt Dip with Veggies

Preparation time: 10 minutes

Cooking time: 0 minutes

Number of servings: 4

Ingredients:

- 1 cup Greek yogurt
- 1 tablespoon lemon juice
- 1 clove garlic, minced
- 1/2 teaspoon dried dill
- Salt and pepper to taste
- Assorted fresh vegetables for dipping (carrots, cucumber, bell peppers, etc.)

Directions:

1. In a mixing bowl, combine the Greek yogurt, lemon juice, minced garlic, dried dill, salt, and pepper. Mix until well combined.
2. Taste and adjust seasonings if needed.
3. Serve the yogurt dip in a bowl alongside the assorted fresh vegetables for dipping.

   Nutritional info: (per serving)

- Calories: 60
- Fat: 0g
- Carbohydrates: 6g
- Protein: 9g

Avocado Salsa

Preparation time: 15 minutes

Cooking time: 0 minutes

Number of servings: 4

Ingredients:

- 2 ripe avocados, diced
- 1 tomato, diced
- 1/4 cup red onion, finely chopped
- 1/4 cup cilantro, chopped
- 1 jalapeño, seeded and finely chopped
- Juice of 1 lime
- Salt and pepper to taste
- Tortilla chips for serving

Directions:

1. In a bowl, gently combine the diced avocados, tomatoes, red onion, cilantro, jalapeño, lime juice, salt, and pepper.
2. Taste and adjust seasoning if needed.
3. Serve immediately with tortilla chips.

Nutritional info: (per serving)

- Calories: 150
- Fat: 13g
- Carbohydrates: 10g
- Protein: 2g

Olive Tapenade on Crostini

Preparation time: 15 minutes

Cooking time: 10 minutes

Number of servings: 6

Ingredients:

- 1 cup pitted Kalamata olives
- 2 tablespoons capers, drained
- 2 cloves garlic
- 2 tablespoons fresh parsley
- 2 tablespoons lemon juice
- 1/4 cup extra virgin olive oil
- Baguette, sliced and toasted

Directions:

1. In a food processor, combine the Kalamata olives, capers, garlic, parsley, and lemon juice. Pulse until coarsely chopped.
2. While pulsing, gradually add the olive oil until the mixture becomes a coarse paste.

3. Taste and adjust seasoning if necessary.

4. Spread the olive tapenade on the toasted baguette slices.

5. Serve as appetizers.

   Nutritional info: (per serving, 2 crostini)

- Calories: 180

- Fat: 10g

- Carbohydrates: 20g

- Protein: 4g

Baked Sweet Potato Fries

Preparation time: 15 minutes

Cooking time: 25 minutes

Number of servings: 4

Ingredients:

- 2 large sweet potatoes, peeled and cut into fries
- 2 tablespoons olive oil
- 1 teaspoon paprika
- 1 teaspoon garlic powder
- Salt and pepper to taste

Directions:

1. Preheat oven to 425°F (220°C).
2. In a bowl, toss the sweet potato fries with olive oil, paprika, garlic powder, salt, and pepper until evenly coated.
3. Spread the fries in a single layer on a baking sheet lined with parchment paper.

4. Bake for 20-25 minutes, flipping halfway through, until the fries are crispy and golden brown.
5. Serve immediately.

Nutritional info: (per serving)

- Calories: 180
- Fat: 7g
- Carbohydrates: 28g
- Protein: 2g

Cucumber Bites with Herbed Cream Cheese

Preparation time: 15 minutes

Cooking time: 0 minutes

Number of servings: 6

Ingredients:

- 2 large cucumbers, sliced into rounds
- 4 ounces cream cheese, softened
- 2 tablespoons fresh herbs (dill, chives, parsley), finely chopped
- Salt and pepper to taste
- Cherry tomatoes or smoked salmon for garnish (optional)

Directions:

1. In a bowl, mix the softened cream cheese with the chopped fresh herbs. Season with salt and pepper.
2. Spread a small amount of the herbed cream cheese on each cucumber round.

3. Top with a slice of cherry tomato or a small piece of smoked salmon if desired.
4. Arrange the cucumber bites on a serving platter.
5. Serve immediately or refrigerate until ready to serve.

   Nutritional info: (per serving, 3 cucumber bites)

- Calories: 70
- Fat: 6g
- Carbohydrates: 2g
- Protein: 2g

Mini Quiches

Preparation time: 20 minutes

Cooking time: 25 minutes

Number of servings: 12 mini quiches

Ingredients:

- 1 refrigerated pie crust
- 4 eggs
- 1/2 cup milk or heavy cream
- 1/2 cup shredded cheese (cheddar, Swiss, etc.)
- 1/4 cup diced cooked ham or bacon (optional)
- 1/4 cup diced bell peppers
- Salt and pepper to taste

Directions:

1. Preheat oven to 375°F (190°C).

2. Roll out the pie crust and cut it into circles to fit a mini muffin tin. Press the crust circles into the tin.
3. In a bowl, whisk together eggs, milk or cream, shredded cheese, diced ham or bacon (if using), diced bell peppers, salt, and pepper.
4. Pour the egg mixture evenly into the prepared crusts.
5. Bake for 20-25 minutes until the quiches are set and lightly golden.
6. Allow them to cool slightly before removing from the muffin tin.
7. Serve warm or at room temperature.

Nutritional info: (per serving, 1 mini quiche)

- Calories: 110
- Fat: 7g

- Carbohydrates: 7g
- Protein: 4g

Conclusion

Your adventure through the world of vegetarian cooking is now complete; please accept my congratulations. As you come to the end of this book, you will not only have experienced a wide variety of recipes, but you will also have acquired a vast amount of knowledge and abilities that will be of great use to you on your continuous journey through the world of cuisine.

Adopting a vegetarian diet is more than just a change in eating habits; rather, it is a deliberate choice to move toward a lifestyle that is both healthier and more environmentally friendly.

You have already made great progress in this direction by being aware of the vast array of tastes, textures, and nutrients that may be obtained from plant-based components.

You have, throughout these chapters, delved into the art of preparing vegetables, learned the alchemy of combining herbs and spices, and experimented with various cooking techniques to create meals that are nourishing as well as delicious. Your kitchen has evolved into a canvas, onto which you have painted dishes that are bursting with color and taste.

You should keep in mind that this is not the conclusion of your voyage through the culinary world as you say goodbye to these pages. Make use of this newly acquired information as a launching point for additional investigation and innovation. You can continue to experience the pleasure of cooking by making adjustments to recipes, developing your distinctive dishes, and shopping for fresh, healthy products.

The power of cooking to bring people together is undoubtedly one of the most enchanting features of this ancient art. Invite your loved ones and close friends to join you on this adventure into the world of flavor by showing them your creations. Gather around the table, take time to savor the food, and focus on making cherished memories that center on the pleasure of enjoying delicious cuisine in the company of wonderful people.

You have contributed to a more sustainable future by deciding to follow a vegetarian diet. Your choice to incorporate more plant-based meals into your lifestyle helps lower your ecological footprint, which contributes to the maintenance of a healthier planet for future generations.

Keep in mind that this book is merely an introduction. There is a whole world of vegetarian cuisine out there waiting for you to discover it, including regional delicacies, flavors from around the world, and novel methods of preparation. Continue to educate yourself, try new things, and find new ways to enjoy the ever-developing world of vegetarian cuisine.

As we part ways, I would like to express my profound appreciation to you for the opportunity to share in your culinary adventure. It has been a privilege to assist you in navigating through all of these pages. I wish for you that your kitchen will always be bustling with joy, inspiration, and the tantalizing scents of scrumptious food fueled by plants.

As you put this book down, I pray that your future endeavors in the kitchen will continue to encourage, edify, and bring happiness not only to you but also to those with whom you enjoy meals. Cheers to an exciting future full of new culinary experiences and the ongoing recognition and appreciation of vegetarian cuisine!

Keep in mind that the doors to the kitchen are always left open and they are awaiting your next culinary adventure. I pray that each dish you cook fills your heart with the love that is shared with others, that your pots bubble over with originality, and that your dishes overflow with vibrant hues.

Printed in Great Britain
by Amazon